Gethsemani Homilies

Gethsemani Homilies

by
Matthew Kelty, OCSO

edited by
William O. Paulsell

Franciscan Press
Quincy University

Gethsemani Homilies by Matthew Kelty, OCSO, edited by William O. Paulsell

Franciscan Press
Quincy University
1800 College Avenue
Quincy, Illinois 62301
Ph. 217.228-5670
Fax 217.228-5672
http://www.quincy.edu/fpress

Book design and typesetting by Laurel Fitch, Chicago, Illinois
Cover design by Jaime Vidal
Frontispiece, cover and chapter-heading woodcuts by Lavrans Nielsen, reproduced by
    permission of the Abbey of Gethsemani

Printed in the United States of America
First Edition: June 2001
First Printing: June 2001
1 2 3 4 5 6 7 8 9 0

Library of Congress Cataloguing-in-Publication Data
Kelty, Matthew.
    Gethsemani Homilies by Matthew Kelty; edited by William O. Paulsell.
    p. cm.
    ISBN 0-8199-0998-X
    1. Catholic Church – Sermons. 2. Sermons, American. I. Paulsell, William O. II. Title.

BX1756.K418 G48 2001
252'.02–dc21   2001033466

For
Timothy Kelly, OCSO
Abbot of Gethsemani, 1973- 2000
With Thanks

Contents

Introduction

 A retreatant stands patiently by the door to the chaplain's office, waiting for a chance to spend a little time with Matthew Kelty. The man or woman, as the case may be, knows that he or she will receive good counsel, given with a sense of humor and a lively spirit from Matthew. The guest house at the Abbey of Gethsemani is always full of people, clergy and lay, Catholic and Protestant, and people of no particular religion at all. The tradition of silence, the beauty of the surrounding, and the haunting chant of the monks in the Divine Offices throughout the day, have a calming effect on people, enabling them to explore their inner depths and search for God on a deeper level than is possible in their normal daily activities.

Father Matthew provides counsel in the afternoons and gives a half an hour talk to retreatants after the last monastic service of the day, around 8:00 P.M. He always begins the talk by reading a few favorite poems by John Milton, Matthew Arnold, Gerard Manley Hopkins, Robert Frost, Thomas Merton, and many others. Then he usually says something about the day, the saint of the day, a particular holiday, or something of astronomical significance such as the summer solstice. He always mentions something about the life of the monk in the monastery, and finally tells some good stories to illustrate his point about how the presence and love of God are always with us. The retreatants hang on every word, for Matthew has a way with words.

He was born in 1915 in Boston, went to public schools, entered the Society of the Divine Word, a missionary order, and was ordained a Catholic priest in 1946. He served the SVD as a missionary in New Guinea and as editor of their magazine, *The Christian Family*. In 1960, he entered Gethsemani and became a Trappist monk.

I knew him in 1970 when he was sent to lead a small experimental community that Gethsemani had taken on in Oxford, North Carolina. I was teaching at a local liberal arts college at the time and often made retreats at Matthew's community. There were never more than three monks there. The idea was that they would live a simple life, support themselves by weaving scarves, ponchos, and other items, and live a life of prayer without having to maintain a large abbey.

Matthew felt a call to solitude, which his superiors at Gethsemani at first resisted. He is a gregarious, outgoing, energetic person, not the usual personality for a hermit. But Matthew felt called to develop the other side of his personality, the solitary, introverted side which few people ever actually saw.

So, after three years at Oxford, he returned to Papua New Guinea, the site of his earlier missionary labors, and lived in a small hermitage for nine years. In 1982, at age sixty-seven, he returned to Gethsemani to resume the community life of a Trappist-Cistercian monk.

The homilies in this collection were delivered at Gethsemani, usually at Sunday masses. Most are brief. They reveal much about the monastic life, but more about the Christian gospel itself.

During one of our annual retreats at Gethsemani my wife, Sally, and I interviewed Matthew for a couple of hours.

WP: Tell us about your growing up in Massachusetts and what led you into the priesthood.

MK: Ours was what you might call a traditional Catholic family. They really didn't know much about the faith. Very simple people, but a profound love for the faith. They loved the church. We didn't make all that kind of money, but we lived in a nice suburb. The church used to print a booklet on how much you gave. They went down Adams street where we lived and listed what everyone gave. My father didn't give all that much, but it was more than most, and he was proud of it.

I always wanted to be a priest, but we never talked about it. I went to a public school so my exposure to the faith was minimal. It wasn't what you would call a thriving parish. It was a beautiful church and all that. I don't ever remember a sermon, but I'm sure there were sermons. There was traditional piety: Stations of the cross during Lent, Sacred Heart devotions during June. That sort of thing. Never a sung Mass; a very modest choir. Today it is quite different. There is now a big staff; then only two priests, a housekeeper, and a janitor.

WP: You saw what the priests did and decided that is what you wanted to do?

MK: No, I didn't want to be a parish priest. At first I wanted to do something with monks, or a religious order. I applied to the Franciscans after high school, but I hadn't had any Latin or Greek, and no money either. The Depression had hit bottom, so they said they were full. The pastor said I should apply at the minor seminary for the Divine Word Society (SVD) down the coast. I didn't know if there were still monks. I knew about them from medieval history, but I thought they were gone. I knew about Jesuits and Franciscans, that's about all. And sisters. There was a monastery in Rhode Island (now Spencer, Massachusetts), but I had never even heard of it. So I signed up at the minor seminary, although I had to go back and do some high school over again. They wouldn't let me pick up the Latin I needed and the Greek I needed and skip the rest. No, they said I should belong to a group. I think they were testing me to see how serious I was. So I stuck it out anyway. Once I got into college and the theologate it was easier.

I wasn't there a year, when they hired a layman, Polish, a shoemaker. His boy was studying in our class, but he didn't persevere. The man was a widower. A year or two later, he went off to the monks in Rhode Island, and stayed too. That's what I wanted to do, but I never pursued it. When I went to college I heard more about it and looked it up and told them I wanted to be a monk. They said, "Oh, you are not monk material." They meant well. They didn't think I had the make-up. So I said, "OK."

Then I went to Techny, the SVD headquarters in Chicago, and was in the novitiate and took vows. I thought, "Well, you can't have two women," so I settled for one, the SVD, and that was it. Off and on through the seminary I would think wistfully about being a monk, but I never did anything about it because they said, "Stay where you are." Then, to rub it in, one of the SVD's from the Philippines, an American, came back and entered here at Gethsemani, with the idea that he would be part of a new foundation from here in the Philippines, which the abbot agreed to because they had lots of monks. He was open to making a foundation. The

Filipinos were annoyed because they were in the most Catholic of all the Asian countries and they were bypassed for monasteries in Japan and other places. The war came, and he gave up because he thought it would never end. Then he came home from Gethsemani, and I think he later went back to the Philippines. When he came home my heart was moved. He was shaven and he was skinny, like a Marine. But he lived to see the monks come to the Philippines. So, it was a kind of secret love affair I had about monks which I used to dream about but never acted on. I never really studied Thomas Merton. I think I read the *Seven Storey Mountain*, I don't really remember, so I wasn't doing anything about this and never visited any monasteries. When I came home from the mission field to Techny, I came through Europe. They took me to one in Germany, but I wasn't impressed because it was a big late Renaissance mansion that was made into a monastery. It wasn't a typical monastery; it looked like a mistake.

I then taught every day and worked on the SVD magazine, a house organ to support the missions, from 1951–1960. It was losing money, but they didn't want to drop it. Then the General, fed up with their procrastination, just decreed by telegram that the magazine is finished, as of now. So we just stopped there and the last issue went through in November. Then I came down here to Gethsemani for I thought, "Here's your chance." I was out of a job. It was like a professor being fired in the middle of the term. So I came down and made a retreat.

WP: This was in 1960?

MK: November, 1959. I had one look and thought, I'll go with this! It had the smell of wet wool mixed with incense. There was no heat, you know, in the house, and they wore wool. The place was damp and the wool smelled like a wet dog. Then there was the daily touch of incense, so there were two attractive smells. Getting up at three o'clock, putting on nice clothes, and singing psalms; that's for me.

There wasn't any screening thing like they have now. They didn't even have a vocation man. I don't know why. Anyway, Merton came over and talked to me for about ten minutes and said, "Well, I guess if you want to come you can come." I thought, "That's enough for me!" They never let on they were interested. You know, it's the diffident style. It's like a woman pretending she's not interested. Of course I was already a priest and had been in religious life for twenty years. It's not like I was just a boy.

WP: What year were you ordained?

MK: Fifty-two years ago, 1946, and I came here when I was forty-five. One of the monks was a psychiatrist, and you know how psychiatrists are, they look at your fingernails and your eyes and then they are reading all kinds of signs. He went through the same routine for five minutes and then said, "Well, I guess if you want to come you can come." And I thought, "Well, I'm coming."

So I was ready to come, but first I had a retreat to give way up in the northern part of Wisconsin to some sisters. I traveled overnight on the train. We were roaring through Illinois about six o'clock in the morning, doing about sixty-five or seventy. There was snow on the ground,and we hit a flatbed truck with three guys in the front seat.

WP: You wrote about that in *Flute Solo* didn't you?

MK: Yes. In those days you couldn't eat or drink before communion, and the first mitigation was you could drink water. Then the second mitigation was you could drink liquids. When you are traveling on a train you go to the dining car early in the morning and, of course, there's nobody there and for a dollar they bring you coffee in a big silver urn and cream and sugar and a rose. It was pure luxury. And the waiter stands there and talks to you. And while we're talking the train shook just like that. So we look out the window three seconds later we see this truck like a toy flying through the air. It was just daylight. The train backed up. There was blood all over the snow; it smelled like a butchershop. I baptized the boy with snow.

The retreat was my last assignment. Then, I was home only a few days and I was going to come, and we had a fire on the 13th of January. I was sleeping in the printing plant and got out just in time. Then I ran through the building. I was naked, just in my underwear, and I stepped on melted hot asphalt from the roof and burned a hole in my foot. Then I had to run across the yard to tell the rest of them about the fire. So all that held me up for a while, but I finally got here in February.

WP: 1960?

MK: Yes. And then when I got here I knew this was the right place for me. It was very difficult because I was forty-five, and by that time you have had a few shabby episodes in your life, and this place could be dreadful. The silence then was total. Now it's palatable; then it was grim. You couldn't talk to anybody, and I didn't know the sign language. The hours in church were longer. The work was harder and the food was poor and the place was cold So it was difficult. In that silence everything in your past from day one goes through your memory. It's very hard because there are no other distractions. Over and over again you think about your past. I used to get so weary. It's like a laundry where you wash your clothes and put them in the dryer and you think that's finally over. It's not over. You do it again. But finally it stops. That's what drives people away from here, the quiet, especially if you are older. Choir is long and it doesn't take all of your attention to sing the psalms. So you are always thinking about the past.

WP: What did you think of your novice master, Thomas Merton?

MK: Well, he was not my type; he was an intellectual. We could never be friends; in fact, I probably wouldn't be friends with any of these monks, and yet there is real love and I am very fond of them. It's beautiful, but it's not that kind of a relationship. It's the difference from having good friends and having your brothers. Both of them are beautiful but they are different. These are not my friends, but they are my brothers, and that may sound funny. Merton would never be my friend because he was all brains and he lived in another world than the one I live in. He was English and I am a Celt, and English are Teutonic. But he was good.

The lasting memory I have of him concerned an incident during Lent. During Lent there is fasting and you get hungry and a little tired and irritable, and impatient. On a dreadful day when it's about twenty-five degrees outside, and a wind blowing in from Canada, he sends you out with a bush hook which is so dull you can't cut anything with it, to cut bushes from the hillside. Really make-do work, cleaning up the hillside. And then the next day with the bright sunshine and crocus beginning to show and spring is coming, and it's fifty degrees outside, just beginning to get warm, and he sends me upstairs to type. I can't type. I hunt and peck and he wants me to type his manuscripts on A.B. Dick stencils. He was never satisfied with what he wrote. He would redo it, he would make a few corrections on this page, but major corrections on the back of the previous page. So you are typing along on this page and then you realize, you forgot the insert. He never shortened; he always expanded, and added whole paragraphs in writing I couldn't read.

It would be all right if you could guess, but if it was proper names you couldn't guess. Appomattox; how do you spell it? You had to know the word. You weren't supposed to bother him after he started working. That was one of his rules. He would be highly concentrated on what he was doing. I would have to go down to his room and knock. I would say, "I can't read your writing," and he would look at me like "Your mother dropped you when you were a baby." He was terrible to work for. I used to dread that.

One day he lines us all up and he goes down the line and he says, "Father Matthew, you will type." I said, "No." And he said, "Father Matthew, you will type." And I said, "No." Then the third time he said, "You will type." "OK," I said, "I will type." No one else would have tolerated that, if you had said "No." It was an order. Three times. I think that was it if I had done it again. The end! I never forgot that. Other monks here still remember that exchange.

But Merton could understand a forty-five year old man who was new and hungry and tired and irritable or whatever and was asked to do something that he found very difficult. He was tolerant enough to appreciate that and to give me a break. Most people wouldn't be bothered. I wouldn't.

WP: Was the fasting more rigorous in those days?

MK: Yes, less to eat. Fasting in my book is a disaster, it just doesn't work for me. You just had coffee and bread in the morning and you dipped the coffee out of a big cauldron. It would be steaming because the refectory had no heat. I was hungry all day. A huge meal at noon of soup and vegetables, but at 2:00 I would be famished. Supper would be a piece of cheese and another piece of bread and some fruit. It was all right; you got enough to eat.

WP: It was breakfast and the evening meal when you fasted?

MK: Yes, one main meal a day was the idea. Only the softies took anything in the morning. That was for the chicken-hearted, those that had no guts. It is the same, only now you can get more in the morning and more in the evening. It's not as grim as it was.

I think a lot of the energy went into staying warm because

most of the house wasn't heated, except the scriptorium. The refectory was cold, and the dormitory was cold, the church had some heat, but it was tough. Anyway, Merton had a sense of compassion and understanding, rather than just treating us officially, if you know what I mean. First of all, he is not a boy; he is an older man.

The novices were an interesting bunch. One was right out of high school, there were two or three priests, one from a religious order and one from a diocese, one was a religious brother. There was one from Ford Motor Company, hired by McNamara so he must have been important. There were a couple of high school graduates; a very mixed group.

WP: Let's go back to Oxford for a minute and talk about solitude. Why did you want to go into solitude?

MK: I was sent to New Guinea as a young priest in 1947. In the Seminary we had to live in community life. Everything was together. We followed the rule of St. Ignatius: "Never alone." When you went on a walk you always had to have someone with you. You were never allowed to touch anyone. You lived this high intensity community life. Then they take you to New Guinea and they put you out in the jungle one hundred miles from nowhere with a Dutchman you saw three or four days a month. We were circuit riders. We had the main station. When I'm home, he's out. Three days here, three days there, making the rounds. Then he'd come home and I'd go out. We would be together just a few days. I almost went crazy with loneliness. You can't talk to primitives. I was there almost three years. I used to have a depression that was almost physical in the afternoons. We didn't have any books or radio. This was right after the World War II.

Anyway, you didn't write home then and tell them, "I don't like it here, bring me home." That just wasn't done. So I went to church one night and said to the Lord, "If I'm not going to make it, get me out of here." I was scared of cracking up or something. About two weeks later we had the annual retreat. It was the one time of the year when everybody got together. The logistics were phenomenal because they had to get these people from all over: horseback, ships, it was quite a maneuver. And we were supposed to keep silence when we got there. Well, we didn't because it was the only time of the year we met. Some priest gave five or six talks a day.

While I'm there the bishop called me aside and he said, "I've got news for you. They want you back in Techny."

I said, "Whose doing is that; yours or theirs?" I figured he might be getting rid of me. He said, "It's theirs." They wanted me to come home and edit this magazine. A friend said, "Tell them you don't want to do it." I said, "I'm glad to do what I'm told." I wasn't that anxious to stay.

So I came home through Europe. That was 1951. The General, the head of the outfit (SVD) asked me, "How do you like your new appointment?" I said, "I think it's a mistake."

I enjoyed community life. After you were ordained the community life was less vigorous. You didn't see that much of one another. The evening recreation after dinner was minimal. Most of the fathers went to the recreation room and read the paper. They had been teaching all day and they weren't interested in sitting down and making idle chatter. But I was, because I was by myself all day. I was in an office with a magazine.

So I came here to Gethsemani because I loved the prayer life and the liturgy life and I wanted a life of prayer and a life of community. Then Merton started talking about solitude. I told him, "I'm not interested. I had that. I know all about it. I've been into it; it's not for me."

But it kept coming up; it was a favorite theme of his. The solitude of the monastic life was in the silence. We are together in solitude. But he, through his studies, maintained that it's not just the silence; it is supposed to be actual, physical solitude for those who want it and are capable of it. And he proved his point. Eventually, the abbot who had opposed him brought it up at the General Chapter and had it passed as legislation, that it was legitimate to have hermits.

Well, after a while I began to give it some thought and understood what he was talking about and then began to take some time out and spend some time alone. I got myself a little hut and spent some time out in the woods and then it was fixed so that I could have a day a week.

WP: That was the pump house below the dam?

MK: Yes. Then finally I began to understand solitude, what it means. I wanted to do it full time. But I didn't want to do it out back of the monastery. You know, if you get married you don't live upstairs. You want to get a house of your own. By that time we had a new abbot and I talked to him for a few months about it. I used to have to talk to him about work, and when we were done with work I would talk about solitude. Finally, I caught on that he wasn't buying it. I finally said, "Will you let me do this?" "No." He said, "If you want to do it, go do it." "With your blessing?" I asked. "No." If I had said, "I am going," he would have said, "How much do you want?" and he would have written me a check. That's the way many abbots operate. Then it's not on their conscience. Their way of thinking, which is not my way of thinking, is that if your conscience tells you to do something, you are supposed to do it, whether you get a blessing or not. For an Irishman, that's no way to operate. What's the point of the vow of obedience if you don't govern your life by it? My theory is that, and I'm sure it's correct, if God gives me the idea, He can surely work through the abbot to confirm it. If He doesn't, there is surely something wrong, and the wrong is probably me. You follow me? That's the way the thing is set up.

Sometimes people want to do something and they go ahead and do it. The abbot doesn't oppose it, but he doesn't bless it, and that way the abbot keeps his hands clean.

Well, anyway, I gave up. Then about three months later he was given the little monastery at Oxford, North Carolina. He didn't have anyone else around who was interested in solitude, at least in whom he had any faith. So, that's where he sent me. It turned out to be providential because it was s superb preparation for what was to come, although I didn't know that at the time. For six months I was there alone. Otherwise, there were only two or three other monks. We always had guests coming. I loved it. I thought it was wonderful. I liked the way we lived it, the style of prayer and Mass.

Then a new abbot was elected. He had no interest in the place, so he gave it away to Spencer. When he came over to make a retreat before becoming abbot he hadn't been there twenty minutes when he said, "Are you still interested in going into solitude somewhere?" We talked about it and I suggested Vancouver where there was a bishop who had a colony of hermits. Then I suggested Ireland where they would never let a hermit starve to death, you know, and New Guinea where I was known. The abbot's council picked Papua New

Guinea, so that's where I went. So it all turned out. Then I had more solitude than I could manage, more than enough. It was good. I stayed there for nine years. It was a nice experience.

When I got to New Guinea, I looked for a place to go and the bishop suggested Bogia, the site of the mission, about a hundred miles up the coast on top of a hill. It is where the mission used to be, and it was all bombed out during the war. After the war the people asked them to move down to the beach, on the shore, which they did. It was beautiful. There was a volcano about ten miles out to sea right in front to me. I could see a hundred miles down the coast. It was just gorgeous.

The bishop said, "Draw a plan and I'll send someone up to build a place for you." It was six months before he came, a youngster from Bristol, England. Meanwhile, I had a little house by the shore at the mission. I lived there alone and ate with the fathers and said Mass and the office by myself and had plenty of time. And that's when I started writing *Flute Solo*, just to get some thoughts on paper. I wrote it during Holy Week, finished Easter Monday. I thought, maybe this will help someone. So I sent it in longhand to a sister I met in North Carolina who lived in Raleigh, and told her that she could probably find someone to type it up. I sent her my Mass money. She sent it to Sheed, Andrews and McMeel, and they turned it down, so it ended up at Gethsemani for the file and I said, "When I die you can read it in the refectory." Two years later, the publisher asked for it back. They wanted to look at it again. The second time they took it. Meanwhile the Gethsemani artist who did these icons left. He was gay and he later caught AIDS. Anyway, when he left he was floundering around and getting nowhere so the publisher went and got him and put him in the art department. He did the cover for my book.[1]

While writing the book I came to terms with myself and was perfectly happy. That made living alone fruitful again because I wasn't unhappy and running away from something. I was able to work out on paper who I was. A solitary experience for that kind of person can be very fruitful because the inner diaologue of the two dimensions of the person, male and female if you want to call them

---

[1] The woodcuts on the cover, the frontispiece and the beginning of each homily in this book are also by this artist, Lavrans Nielsen.

that, is very strong and the personal enterprise then becomes very healthy and good. You see, most people work out the relationship, the dynamics of their male and female sides through external marriage and through the marriage learn to come to terms with their other side. Sally teaches you how to come to terms with your total person and she from you and then later you grow into persons who are totally integrated and now the love is different, now you love each other's person, not needing one another but enjoying one another. Because it is through one another that each have attained to full development as persons. It's not just a psychological thing, because a person is the one who is capable of your love. Up until that stage the person is just on the way. Christ, therefore, is the model not just for men but for women, too, because he is not a male, he is a person and we love him as a complete integrated person. Our culture stresses toughness, masculine, you know, the men are supposed to be tough and women are supposed to be child-brides. Well, it was the women who revolted first and said, "We are not child-brides, we are people." Men are finally beginning to catch on.

In the monastic context it works out very healthily that way because we do a lot of feminine things, so-called: wash dishes, serve one another, take care of the sick, set the table, wash the clothes, clean the house, all things usually associated with women. At the same time, we earn our living, make an income, pay the taxes, you know, do all the male things. So there is both, not just one or the other. Now sisters, nuns, are moving over into administration, running huge hospitals, universities, orphanages. It takes not merely maternal capacities but masculine authoritarian capabilities, and then doing it alone intensifies it. That's why celibacy can be healthy, why it isn't sick. I never wanted to be married, it never occurred to me, because I had more woman in me than I could handle. I don't need another one. For a kid this is terrible when you are growing up and everyone is into seeking girls. You know the high school talk; it didn't mean a thing to me. I mean women are interesting, but as far as sexual objects, that meant nothing to me. So you begin to realize that something is wrong, somewhere. Then when I got into seminary they used to talk about girls and I used to think, well, their vocations are pretty wishy-washy, not very strong. I never had any of that interest. It didn't occur to me, of course, what it meant.

SP: Do you remember when you visited Atlantic Christian College and one of your lectures was on the anima and the animus? I wondered if that was when you were beginning to work out your own identity.

MK: Yes, I was reading Jung then. I started reading him here. Jung was still very unpopular in those days because he was the first psychiatrist to say that religion had anything to do with psychiatry. Most of them said it was a No-No. People called him a mystic. They didn't mean it in a flattering sense; they meant he was a fake. To counteract that the Bollingen Foundation, I don't know who it is, translated all his works and had them published and sent them to psychiatrists. They came out in great big volumes, bound in black, looked very mysterious. There were about twenty volumes, a big set, in a section of the library just for priests. It was considered a bit dangerous. That's the way it was in those days. I was in the library one day and I see this big set of books. I had never heard of the man. I saw these books and I was fascinated and I started to read him at random. It did me as much good as Merton. He took traditional monastic terms and structures and translated them into psychological language.

We speak psychological language; we don't speak the language the fathers of the church spoke. The church fathers used a different kind of language. It can just go by you and it doesn't jell, it doesn't click. Whereas Jung talks in psychological language; that's where we are, that's where we live. And he would use terms like anima and animus, terms that you could grasp. That started here, and I was already into it when I went to Oxford. I had talked to Juniors here about what I knew about it, and then at Oxford it worked out.

The experience in New Guinea as a hermit was different from the first time because I wasn't an official ecclesiastic, so the people related to me differently. They like priests and brothers and sisters, they like the Church, they don't have any argument, but you're still an official, where this time I was just a guy on the hill. I had no official capacity, so they could be very free with their language. I discovered things I didn't know about them, and that is that the men are extremely affectionate and warm and friendly among themselves. However, in the presence of Europeans they put their hands down and act (by our standards) very normal because they know that American and European men don't touch. So when they were in our presence they never did. When I was by myself and got to know them, I discovered that they loved to touch and embrace, and kiss among themselves. So I took to being affectionate with them. Oh, dear God, it wasn't sexy, it was just affection. To kiss them would be overwhelming because no European male ever kissed them and they would be so happy and would think, "He is just like us." It was very touching because we as a culture are very European. We can't be any other way. We are colder and they are not. They don't understand it. They are real sharp. Like any people who have been subdued, they learn what is acceptable and what is not to the governing power. So they are careful not to do anything that doesn't look right. That was a real eye-opener. Then I realized that they are probably healthier than we are in the sense that they are more uninhibited in their affection for each other. I don't know how you get people like the Poles and people like John Paul II. I saw two films in New Guinea in German, one on John Paul and one on Mother Theresa. Every person that John Paul would talk to he would touch. Touch, touch, touch. And Mother Theresa was the same. Wherever she went she always touched the people. The monks aren't very affectionate. When I came back from New Guinea, having been away for nine and a half years I was kissing the monks because I was very glad to see them. They would go along with it, but they were a little bit uncomfortable. After about a month of that I realized that cultural patterns are different here. They were very nice about it, but most preferred a handshake.

WP: Are there other things you learned in solitude?

There is darkness and evil and ugliness, and the capacity and tendency for that is present in the human. That is something you confront in quiet. Not only personal sinfulness, but an awareness of a deeper sinful dimension or capacity for it in the human. In other words, the unconscious has to be redeemed, has to be saved by Christ. Unless that is done the conversion isn't really complete. There is kind of a cosmic dimension to evil so that the monks' participation in the search for good and for God isn't easy. You discover that you are kith and kin not only to holy people but also to sinful people who get caught up in ugliness and violence and the sins of the world. That, too, has to be redeemed somehow.

WP: I have heard other people say that in solitude they feel closer to the human family.

MK: Yes, that's another way of putting it. You realize in your own personal history that you are not all that different given a change of circumstances. So compassion rises in your heart and you become really loath to point a finger at anyone. You realize what you would do under similar circumstances. So it makes you more merciful.

People avoid quiet because the first confrontation is personalized in their own lives and they back off. It's kind of foolish because if you're not that absorbed in the mercy of God you don't get anywhere. But if you move further on, the idea of participation in the whole drama of salvation becomes very real. And that would be the heart of this place. It's not just a personal salvation trip; it becomes an engagement with the whole picture, the whole program. I call the monastic life an art form. It is a way of expressing a Christian truth that is slightly exaggerated just as most art is a little bit overdone, not too much, just a little exaggerated and people get it. They understand that it's an art form. Not everybody has to be a monk, but they know what a monk is saying and they are able to agree with it.

WP: I disagree with you in your comparison of yourself with Merton. You are an intellectual.

MK: But I had no intellectual training, let's put it that way.

WP: You read, you write, you think deeply. You are an intellectual.

MK: Well, I never thought of it that way. Some people find someone like me who thinks haphazardly and intuitively, juvenile. We have someone here that I call a real intellectual. He has been educated and trained and disciplined and he has a lot of knowledge.

WP: You are a self-educated intellectual.

MK: Yeah, you pick up things along the way here. Well, I enjoy being what I am. I don't feel bad about it. When I see some intellectuals I think, God help us. I have God in my life and I have everything I want. I know I had nothing to do with it.

WP: Tell us about the major changes here that have taken place at Gethsemani since you came here.

MK: It's nicer. It's more gentle, more kind, more tolerant. I think the old regime was good and it worked and they liked it but I think its time had come. It was very rigorous and it produced a bunch of tough men. Because it was tough they were under pressure and it was hard. You don't have much tolerance under pressure. Short tempers. You know food, everything, the whole total program, was difficult. It produced holy people, no question. Any kind of suffering will. Over the years it has become more kind. The abolition of the Chapter of Faults[2] changed the whole contour. It's one thing to accuse yourself; quite another to accuse others. You are aware that people are watching you, and then you are watching others to catch some fault. You had to have something to say, you can't just show up week after week and not say anything. You were made to feel guilty if you did not take part in the exercises, so you had to find things to say. You can see what that does to a community.

WP: When did that go out?

MK: In the sixties, the major changes came with Vatican II. We didn't think in negative terms about our life. It was just the way things had been; that's just the way they were. There was love all right. You have to be pretty good to pull back and say this is not right.

    I used to talk to the brothers with sign language. There really wasn't much communication. You certainly couldn't just sit down and talk to anyone. The brothers got very proficient at signs. It's not a language like sign language is, you could never teach with it. It's pragmatic, practical, but it was very useful and I compared it to a hum of bees. There was a hum in the community with signs. It was esoteric, exotic, it was strange. No one else could do it, only monks had this secret language. The brothers were good at it because they were with each other all day, and they were communicating day and night, and that relieved a lot of pressure. It also created problems. There was a lot of misunderstanding from misreading signals. But I thought it was a real benefit because it released pressure. When the

---

[2]   The Chapter of Faults was an ancient monastic custom, a meeting of the community in which several monks accused themselves of external fautls (such as being late, breaking silence, damaging community property) which they might have committed. They received a penance from the Abbot. After the self-accusations were over, any monk who had noticed an unacknowledged fault in another brother could accuse him before the community. Serious faults were of course reserved for the privacy of the confessional.

monks started talking they couldn't control it and there was talking everywhere. So we had a fake kind of silence.

Most seminaries and religious orders in those days, and to some extent now, had hours and times of silence. After night prayer there was silence, and it was rigorous. You weren't supposed to communicate. A smile was considered out of order. You were to stay out of each other's hair. There was a funny side to sign language. You could look out your window and follow a conversation down in the courtyard. Then when they dropped the rigid practice of silence, the monks had to learn how to be quiet. It didn't take long. They realized that the house couldn't have talking everywhere and they settled down. So we have a quiet place. There is no talking in your room or the corridors or the library or the scriptorium or the refectory, church, sacristy. But they talk at work, small talk, chatter, some of them. It's not bad. And there are little clusters: the kitchen crew, the fruitcake crowd, bakers. There are little groups. I am isolated over here in the Guest House. So I don't get the news or what's going on. I have to go look for it. I go by the kitchen sometimes just to see what's new. Otherwise you can get very isolated. Then you can always take a walk with somebody, too, so it's much better. Still, it's not slack. The tone of the place is good. You never hear ugly words or snapping at each other.

That used to happen, well, you know, when men get under pressure. We just had a lot of crazy customs. The choir used to be much bigger, maybe it was harder to handle, I don't know, and of course everything was in Latin. The choirmaster would walk up and down the choir with little signs that said, "Slow down the ending, not so fast, soften the ending," stuff like that. Sometimes the monks would be touchy and irritable in choir because people were dragging or they were too fast or whatever. The hours in church are not as long now, not as tedious. Sometimes the tone was set too high, like Solesmes, and we sounded like a bunch of eunuchs. Everything was high. When you were done with Matins your throat would be sore because it was supposed to sound ethereal and angelic. Awful. They don't do that anymore.

In the past they worked much harder and longer, morning and afternoon and harder physical work. For ten years we tore the building down; it was hard physical labor. The choir monks worked on the building. The brothers had their own work to do. Tearing it up and replacing it with steel. So, it's toned down a lot. And then we had all these meetings, dialogues and committees. And all kinds of stuff in the wash of Vatican II.

Finally, the showdown came. One of the monks acted as the overseer. He put the place on its feet financially. He was a genius. He had a handsome herd of Holstein, the dairy, he updated the whole operation, it was all made scientific, and then the whole business of fruitcake and cheese and advertising, he was into engineering and farming and agriculture. There were a lot of competent people here. Then we got into alfalfa and that whole business. Then pigs, we raised pork and we sold country ham and bacon, all mail order. The monks worked very hard. Merton was a big one for saying, "Cool it." General Motors for Jesus is not the idea. Too much. They finally confronted the overseer and said, "How much would we have to work to make it." He said, "If you work four hours a day we can make it." So that's what toned everything down.

Then, we got a new abbot. You remember the gift shop? The monks hated it. Bus loads of ladies came out from Louisville. At that time we were on the Gray Line tour along with my Old Kentucky Home, Jim Beam, the Cathedral, Abraham Lincoln's birthplace. They would wind up here at 2:00, attend the service of None, and then go down to the gift shop, buy stuff and go home. Almost daily. There were tours in the monastery. All the retreatants would go through the place on Wednesdays and Saturdays. It was like a zoo, you know. There were big groups in those days.

Anyway, once it was decided that we didn't need to work that hard, that there was no point in it, the afternoons were free. We worked in the morning. Some chores were in the afternoon: kitchen, setting tables, that kind of stuff. And then there was some work in the afternoon. If you wanted to work you could. But the tone of the place quieted down, it was less hectic. A former abbot used to say, "You want to be like the poor, do what the poor do, they work hard." The shift came, when the next abbot just turned everything off. He wasn't interested. He turned all the money over to the monks. I think he learned later that you had to be more cautious. But many of the monks were capable. They gave money away because they thought we had too much. You remember in the sixties there was much concern about the third world, and the poor, and minorities. Stashing money away was considered unethical, so they gave a lot away. They didn't waste it. But when the next abbot wanted to rebuild the Guest House they didn't have any money. So they went to our retired abbot and said, "Would you go to some of your friends for money to remodel the Guest House?" He knew he had left a lot of money when he retired, but most of it had been given away. Anyway, we got by.

There is a beautiful room upstairs in the library that has an open vaulted ceiling. It's the scriptorium, a room with a wonderful view. At the end of the wing is a little chapel, like a miniature choir with choir stalls. Before, when we were still in Latin, the abbot had the office translated into English, maybe except Matins, exactly as we had it. It was Latin and English together. They were doing it when I came. In fact, I had to read proof for the text. The brothers, maybe seventy-five, all went to this choir and did the offices in English in anticipation. The abbot knew that down the road English was coming for everybody. That went on for about ten years. He had hoped that all the brothers would move from that over to the regular (priest) choir when the change to English came. But they didn't. They said, "We're not into this office business." Some of them did, maybe half of them. In the old days everybody in the choir was a priest. The abbot hoped the brothers would move en masse. Some houses had a lot of trouble because the brothers didn't want to become choir monks. They wanted to keep their lifestyle because they liked it.

WP: I remember coming to an office here almost forty years ago when everybody was present.

MK: Brothers came to Sunday Vespers and Sunday Lauds and Compline every night. They sang along with us. They sang by memory without knowing what they were singing.

WP: Do you still have Brothers that don't come to choir.

MK: Oh yes. That's the first question that people ask, "How many are you?" Oh, about seventy, seventy-five. "Well, where are they?" Some are sick and some of them say Our Father, Hail Mary offices, or say the psalms by themselves. They work it out with the abbot. Technically, if they entered as brothers you can't change the system on them in mid-life. So most of the younger brothers enter and simply go to choir. Even if they can't sing they go along with it. For most of the young ones entering today, that's what a monk is. You go to choir, you go to work and you read your books.

SP: We saw pictures of how you used to sleep in cells.

MK: Yes, that has changed, we have private rooms now. That was another big help because you had no place to go. You couldn't go to the dormitory during the day. It was only for sleep. Merton always had a cubicle in a corner someplace because he couldn't stand snoring and some of them snored. If you are tired enough you just go to sleep, but he couldn't. He was too restless. And they never opened a window all winter. It smelled like wet wool because it was cold. There was no heat. And when it gets cold it gets damp. And you had huge blankets, and you wore your clothes to bed, wool. Everything was together. You read books together, you had your desk, you had a scriptorium, the brothers had a scriptorium, Now it's a reading room.

WP: What kind of reaction was there when they dropped Latin here.

MK: Oh, they couldn't wait! They were glad. When I came here I had grown up in a Latin background. I thought it was beautiful. I liked the big Latin books. I hadn't been here but a month or two when I heard them talking about when are we going to get rid of it? Get rid of it! I thought they were out of their minds. Why would you get rid of it? Oh, they couldn't wait, and there were all kinds of rumors. First it was going to be the Mass, and then it was going to be active orders and so on, and even the Benedictines would change, but our monks would keep their Latin. Finally, all that was left was the contemplatives that don't have an active ministry, and Paul VI pled with the Cistercians to keep the Latin. Somebody should keep it and sing it. "No," they said, "No way. We're not a museum. What do you think we are, a relic?" There are a few places in Europe, and the Common Observance Cistercians, some of those houses, still do it.

WP: I was at a Common Observance house in Dallas and they did it.

MK: Yes, they didn't change it. And some houses in Europe where there is more of a Latin background. It wasn't all that high quality music; some of it was pretty mediocre, but every now and then there were some beautiful things. They used that Latin Psalter for a thousand years. Jerome translated it. That was traditional with the monks. The Vulgate. Some of the melodies were very old and go way back into the time of Ambrose and those people.

WP: How about the choirmaster, did it bother him?

MK: Oh, I'm sure, it was a heartbreak. He didn't reveal it though. He didn't have time, he had to create the new liturgy. He is a genius. Sometimes he was only two days ahead of us. He writes beautiful hymns, he does lovely hymns. He never has his name on them, only CW. Then he wrote all of those antiphons we use now. If he hadn't been for him, who knows where we would have been. The change was so fast. I used to ask him about it. Couldn't we sing a little Latin piece once in a while? But he never expressed his feelings.

Old Father Andrew used to say the office in Latin in addition to the English one. When he died, I said to the choirmaster, "Why don't you give him an old Latin funeral?" But he wouldn't do it. He wouldn't make a concession. But the new choirmaster will sing something in Latin once in a while. Now we have a whole generation that doesn't know Latin.

SP: I thought you did Mass this morning with flair.

MK: Yeah, I like it. I enjoy doing Mass.

WP: Would you encourage a young fellow to become a monk today?

MK: Oh yes, if he has any gifts for it. Now and then they come by. I suppose half of it is romantic. They like the liturgy, rubric, clothes. The life is still pretty ritualized, eating together all dressed up, and in a very particular mode, you know, sitting in choir, and I like all that. And that then becomes the platform, the staging place, that gets you started. The idea is to shake you free of the ways of the world, worldly clothes, not that that's sinful and evil, but it's worldly, but you drop all that and live another way. They do the same thing in the military; they give you different clothes, different protocol, rituals of all kinds, salutes. That becomes the platform against which the thing can take off. So our way makes possible an engagement with the world of the spirit. For some the style is as far as it goes. But that's standard. You know, you may have a hundred people that write poems, but one may actually be a poet. It takes the hundred to produce the one. The same with artists or singers or whatever. If you don't have all these mediocre ones you don't get the outstanding ones. So they are not mediocre in the sense that their contribution is very real.

WP: What does it take today to make a good vocation?

MK: I think the faith is dying and I don't know why. I think the church today, surely the monastic life, is in better shape than it has ever been. We have good popes, good bishops, good priests, and beautiful buildings. Everything is there and I don't know why the faith is dying. I don't know what is going on. The monastic life has never been in better shape. It's as good now as it has ever been. It does have a few crazies, a lot of weird qualities.

Why, all of the sudden, are there no priest vocations here? I have theories. Once is noise. I think their imagination is killed by constant input. Disney ruined fairy tales by putting them on screens. It's all passive, where before you read it and you imagined Cindrella and the pumpkin. And then they get constant input, getting more and more interesting and fascinating and more and more of it from dawn to dark. There is no silence, no time to ponder or reflect on anything and in that context religion dies.

What did people in this part of Kentucky do around here all day in the past? Nothing. For a long time there was no TV, no radio, no phonograph. Out in the fields all day it was quiet. What did they do for excitement? Go down and see the train twice a day, who gets on who gets off and pick up the mail. Made their day. Well, then they would be pious people, raised against a background of religion and they were Catholic and they went to Mass every Sunday and celebrated the feasts, the cycle of the year, so they had things to think about, and baptisms and weddings and funerals, you can see how emotion arises out of that kind of a background. I'm not condemning it, but it doesn't get into the kind of thing that produces poets.

The monastic life should be poetic, romantic, artistic, and introverted. Does it have any common sense? Extroverts want to serve God. They would do something. The world, God knows, is in trouble and needs help. And if you come here and spend your time singing the psalms and making fruitcake, it's crazy. Except, if you are an introvert, it isn't. Making cheese and fruitcake is just something that makes the contemplative life possible, you know, pays the bills. For us, the real world is within. That doesn't make us a superior people, it is just who we are.

As a western culture, we are extroverts, and if you are not an extrovert, honey you won't make it. So you acquire extrovert ways if you haven't got them. If your boy grows up and becomes 18 and you ask him what he's going to do and he says he going to be a poet, you ask, "What are you going to do for a living." The best they can do is do what you do, where you can teach and engage in something very high quality and it pays the bills.

WP: Our youngest daughter majored in philosophy and every body asked, what are you going to do with that?

MK: Yeah, what are you going to do? How are you going to earn a living?

WP: What kind of qualities in a person would make a good vocation here?

MK: You need to have a feeling for art and beauty and ritual, ceremony, and then, of course, a love for God, and a desire to commit yourself and give yourself away and abandon family life. It gives you a community where you can share a life of love, and it's disciplined and ascetical and that prevents it from becoming, you know, inverted. And meanwhile you help build something very beautiful, a city of peace and love and it's a great benefit to the world. Even if monks are romantic, they are always very practical. They were the first capitalists of Europe, building up businesses.

Today we get some inquiries, but every now and then someone who wants to be a monk and would obviously make a good monk comes by and we start asking a few impertinent questions. Well, he has a child up in Minneapolis; wouldn't that cause a few problems? Well, no, his mother has him. Then the other thing is that they owe thousands to the government for their education. It's so easy.

You know, people don't seem to marry anymore. They just live together. It's not good preparation for this place. Of course, being chaste and celibate in that world is asking a good deal. Then many of them are disenchanted with the church. They are not what we used to be, traditional Catholics who loved the church and that was it. The church has changed. Then they get mad at the local pastor, which is the church locally. They don't fight the bishop or the pope, they do it at home. Catholics don't give the way Protestants do. They support the church and they support religious orders, but they don't give like Protestants, as they used to. That's a sign that something is not right. There may be nothing critical said at home about the church, but the kid picks it up, that being a priest is not at the top of the list. It's way down on a list, so it's not the first thing that enters their head. A monk goes home and his nieces and nephews don't know beans about the church. They see the church as something nice if you like it. Nothing against it. The Pope is just wonderful. Everybody thinks Mother Theresa is just wonderful, but that's it. We have been through all this before. So you just hang on and make do and hope better times will come.

WP: I used to hear people say that if someone was a good monk, he was a good community person.

MK: Yes, it would be essential. You have to like people because there is a type that thinks this is a good place to get away from people, but it's the worst place to come for that. Being a solitary won't work unless you can live in community. If you can't live with community you will never be able to live with yourself. Some think the problem is everybody else, all these creeps I have to live with. Well, the biggest creep is yourself. Those who don't know that never last when they do come here.

WP: So, how do you see the future here?

MK: Positively, with qualifications. We Cistercians have been around nine hundred years. Looking at the statistics, it's a roller coaster, so it's just a matter of hanging on, that's all. This drop in vocations will pass; the monastic life will come back. In the third world it's different. In Indonesia, Africa, and Asia, the monastic life is doing very well. They have the faith. You don't feel like your are just wasting time; you feel like it's a contribution to the world in terms of faith. You haven't retired to the country in order to nurse your wounds. It's a viable form of life; I would say it's as good as anything that's going on. And you need poets, and dramatists and singers and dancers and artists and monks. They are not practical. We were just reading today that Joseph II, emperor of Austria, threw out all of the contemplatives, closed their houses, took their property, put them on pensions, and got rid of them because they weren't practical. He would be typical of many people's mentality. When one of our abbots first entered here as a monk, his mother wrote and asked that he not be admitted. She thought he should do something practical like some kind of active ministry.

Yes, I have hope for the future. I'm not depressed. The monks aren't either. They have a sense of history. We are living in a house that has been here for one hundred and fifty years. So it drops in numbers; we keep going.

WP: Give us a summary of what Christian faith is. What is the gospel for you?

MK: To me it is the presence of God everywhere and in everything. That comes naturally for a Celt. Even as a child I could find God easily. And I can remember as a child wondering why people weren't nice when God was so good. I was already aware of the difficulties in the human situation: poverty and violence and human sinfulness. Why does this happen when the beauty of God, is seen so clearly in nature and trees and birds, the things a kid is aware of. We always lived near the sea, and the ocean is wonderful for that openness to God. Loving your neighbor and so on follows from knowing the beauty of God. And the coming of Christ and his having pity on us. He came and joined us to get us to do good and he paid for it, but he turned it into joy. That made sense. I defend the missionaries, but that's not where I'm at. I can go out and preach the gospel, but it wasn't a passion for me the way it is for the pope. I would much sooner stay home and pray about it and think about it. More intro-vert than anything. My sister was an extrovert and she was more male than I was, more outgoing, more aggressive. She would stand up to my father and mother. When they gave an order she didn't like she would defy them, but I was just the opposite. I was easy to please. Whatever they said I did. I just held my anger in, put up with it. Aggression doesn't come naturally to me. In high school competition was useless. I'm not that way; I don't know how. I had no ability in sports, which for a kid is devastating. I couldn't hit a ball, I couldn't do anything. I did single things: skate and run and swim and row a boat, but never competitively. Didn't know how to do it. That's a curse for a boy. So, actually, the SVD was good for me, even though not exactly my cup of tea. It forced me to be an extrovert, to engage and get involved. As long as it was sports I was hopeless, but when I got into college, I was editor of the paper, and I could act, and I could sing so I was always in the choir. I could get by on that. That makes you a valid member of the community. You didn't have to deal with basketball and baseball. So that's why I had a really happy time. So I edited the paper and put on plays.

I don't enjoy encounter and conflict. I go to pieces. I don't know how to do it. So you develop the skills, but they are false, artificial. They are contrived. Well you can do that at twenty-five and thirty and it's all right, but by the time you are forty it's different. Like when I was in New Guinea you sit down at the table for breakfast and you say, "I hear the bishop is getting a helicopter." Someone says, "Who told you that?" "Well," I say, "Let's see, who told me that. One of the brothers told me." The reply? "I knew that two weeks ago." You have a fight on your hands. I was just trying to be pleasant. But they like that, they enjoy it. Then when I came here, I took one look at the monks, you know, three o'clock in the morning, putting on pretty clothes and singing psalms, that's for me. You could see they were gentle, even then. And it got better all the time. But the preliminary of it was good for me because it forced me to develop another side too, so in a way it was providential. It's been a good trip.

1 ~ Monastic Life

Beyond Gender

Although I never experienced it, I have heard from several of a phenomenon in earthquake country, such as along the major fault that runs through the South Pacific. One day, Australian volunteer John Hickey was working with the cattle in the plantation: thousands of tall, majestic palms like cathedral pillars in rows miles long, beneath in high grass are cows munching, mooing moodily to one another. The air is noisy with the cries of birds whose voices are as wretched as their plumage is gorgeous. All of a sudden there is perfect stillness. No cow moves, no bird calls. The change is startling. It is a silent church. Then, ten, twenty seconds later, the terrifying shake of the earth beneath you, a pan of jello held by a nervous cook.

I think of that in these mysterious days of silence after Ascension, before the coming of the Spirit in power. So, too, before a tropical storm, the mad mix of orange and green and mauve clouds swirling dangerously, the suspicious lightness of the air, the hush, the hesitancy. And then before you know what has happened, the sky is black, and there comes a roaring gale of torrents of driving rain. A wild scene up out of nowhere. And it is all over in ten minutes. We are now in that hesitant edge, the moment when nothing happens and everything is about to. The great breakers rolling to shore, lips pursed, tons of water about to spill.

They are three: the Father, the Son, the Holy Spirit. There is a modality that goes with each, a quality. Maybe we can muse a moment on mystery which no words can speak, no symbol signify.

Because we seem to be a patriarchal society, we tend to think of our religion as patriarchal. I am not so sure it is, though I assume we are. We do call him Holy Father, after all, Pope John Paul. Papa Noster. It would be just a significant to call him Brother John Paul, Frater Noster.

We have taken to calling the priest Father, though Brother is nice, maybe nicer.

The first way of seating in church is as in a hall, in a theater, a classroom. All in neat rows facing toward the action, the source, at the elevated front. It goes well with God the Father, asserts the male principle, the idea of authority, control, truth, order, law and grace. For many, this is the Catholic Church, impregnable champion of orthodoxy, the greatest and oldest organization on the face of the earth. They way most of our churches are arranged says that. You tell us. We listen. We learn. We obey. And so we love and are loved.

Monks favor another way. We love God, but we know that love of God is one with love of neighbor. The truth is not in us unless we embrace both God and brother. So we face one another in God, in choir, in chapter, in refectory. This is no trifle. We take care to emphasize it. We are in constant living communion with our brother and so we know that we are face to face with God.

Because love of God and of brother means both toughness and tenderness, courage and tolerance, suffering and dedication, we are one with a Jesus who is not male principle, not female principle, but both: integrated, total human, perfect human. No artist ever sculpted a tough Jesus, painted a macho Lord. He is always tough tenderness, vulnerable strength. Model priest, prophet, poet, Christian, for all, young and old, male and female, single and married. The universal one. To monks religion is not patriarchal. It is fraternal, communal, brotherhood.

When we come to the Eucharist, it is something else again. Here we gather in a great circle around the altar, the center of the universe, the heart of all that is. In a great ring around the stone of sacrifice, priests and people are one with the angelic choirs who surround the throne of the Eternal God singing undying praise. This is the work of the Holy Spirit. This is feminine fruition, the fulfillment of the dream. The gifts of the Spirit complete: understanding, knowledge, wisdom, counsel, piety, fortitude, fear. And the fruits of the Spirit: charity, joy, peace, patience, benignity, goodness, mildness, faith, modesty, continence, chastity. These follow the following of Jesus, prove its genuineness, Christianity lived, the Church vibrant with holiness, rich in the Spirit. In this earthly prelude we are joined in perfect love and so face God in total joy. It is a foretaste of the Kingdom.

Massive spectacles in great bowls and domes and stadiums are a gathering around a contest, highly stylized, often a kind of ballet. We ought not to miss the reason for the great pull these events have. They represent far more than is evident. They reveal unspoken hungers and thirsts and longings. They are a sort of lay liturgy of the struggle of good and evil, some subtle hint of the cosmic engagement in which we are all engaged. The stakes are eternal life.

When we gather around the altar to ponder and share the conflict of good and evil in the passion and death and rising of Jesus, we await the Spirit He promised, the Spirit that calls us beyond docility to the Master, beyond engagement in loving dialog with brother and sister, to the final wholeness which is all creation ringed in a dance of love before Almighty God: Father, Son, and Holy Spirit.

Talking with God

 I suppose it will not be too long before we have a computer screen at each desk in choir, with some central station that will program an Odd week and an Even week, complete with hymns, psalms, readings, and prayers. Then all, guests too, will have the right page and correct text, all without benefit of overhead light. So a soft blue will suffuse the choir, rather than, say, lights that make it look like high noon at night Vigils.

There is really nothing particularly remarkable in this, at least as an adaptation to choir stalls. It would be a marvelous achievement, though no more remarkable than a printed page replacing a hand-lettered one, or even books at all, as compared with monks who knew the psalter by heart. What is remarkable is that the thing should be there at all. We by familiarity may be much unaware of the wonder we are witness to.

We are accustomed to the fact that there is a group of men talking to God. Talking to God is prayer. The talk involves praise, adoration, thanks, petition, sorrow. Monastic prayer is prayer of a very particular sort, prayer that is a matter of total involvement. Here is no mere quiet, interior prayer—necessary to be sure—but prayer in common, in public. Brothers praying together to God. Aloud. In a special setting: not merely a church, but a monks' choir in a monks' church. They are vowed life-long to God. They are in costume. The music is special. They form a hallowed tradition some fifteen thousand years old, laid out in great detail by St. Benedict, the father of western monasticism. He began all this and it has never ceased. What else in the world is like it? Surely, only the sacraments of Holy Church surpass it. Granted that styles in the sacraments have changed some over the years, but they have not changed *that* much. There is a basic reality here that perseveres, and it is rooted in a Psalter that pre-dates Christ, as we post-date him.

If we were to witness a choir of the deaf at the worship of God in the prayer of the Church, the Liturgy of the Hours, we would perhaps capture the impact we once sustained when we first encountered this scene. For the deaf could also line up in choir, take the places and change the dialogue of prayer by way of the psalms through sign language. Now this side, now that, bowing at the Gloria, sitting for the reading. It would be the silence that would strike us, the intensity of the communication from one choir to another. Brother praises God with brother. Mankind at prayer. As mankind, as brotherhood, as community, as Church. We would be struck by the beauty of the silent scene, and thus aware that as humankind, we pray.

While we can commune with God as with another in heart and mind and will, and surely reach the depths of the human heart and the heart of God, our usual manner of commerce is through sign and symbol, through word spoken and gesture made, through vesture and rite, stance and posture, holy place and holy setting. We know and love the God of rain and of the starry night, of mountain and valley in bloom. But we need also to talk to God in words, make love to Him through body, and find exceeding joy in doing so with others. We are family, community, and a family gathers before fireplace, around the table, at the altar.

St. Benedict left to the West, to the world, a tradition of prayer, prayer of great beauty, prayer rooted in the mysteries of Christ's birth, his life and work, his death and rising, his sending of the Spirit and the founding of the church to continue until his coming again at the end. It is total prayer in its sense of community and its being involved with every dimension: sound, sight, speech, song, ritual, vestment, setting. All that awakens in us this truth, that the life of faith is the same. God permeates, penetrates in all we do—work, reading, service, leisure. God is part of all, in all, and in all we love and serve Him.

It would no doubt take us by surprise if we should open the door of a church and once inside note a double line of men deep in prayer, expressed in sign exchanged back and forth across a choir. In silence. Its beauty would overwhelm us, men talking to God with one another.

No less awesome the sound of music, of chant, of psaltery, of men at prayer together for the joy of it, the glory of it, for one another, for the world, because there is a God. God be praised for this great gift so unmerited. That this fragile beauty should perdure is a marvel of God's providence, and we are grateful. A gratitude more profound for our being called to be part of it, however unworthy; to be called to help make it possible, for it is a community enterprise. We are gathered by grace from here and there, for some long years ago, for some not long ago at all, and gifted for this splendid enterprise for the good of all mankind in Christ Jesus our Lord. Praise be God for St. Benedict and for all who follow him. Amen.

Communication

Communication is a first fruit of the coming of the Holy Spirit.

In 1843, Samuel Morse obtained use of the right-of-way along the new Baltimore and Ohio Railroad, between Baltimore and Washington, to erect wire for his telegraph. A year later this first message was tapped out, one letter at a time, "What hath God wrought." It was thought a marvel, and it was. Ever after there was a telegraph office in every railroad station. Communication is a most significant aspect of the human scene. We speak naturally, and from the dawn of speech we extend the faculty to unimagined dimensions.

Indian trails, waterways by river and canal, highways and throughways are a web covering the nation. From telegraph to telephone to radio to television to facsimile to electronic networks by cable and satellite, instant communication is possible to almost anywhere when a superb mail system will not suffice. We do love to stay in touch. From clay tablet to papyrus to parchment to paper, the written, printed word is endlessly multiplied. It must be in the nature of our kind to communicate.

It is the nature of God Almighty, too. So it is a god-like gift. The inner communion of God we call the mystery of the Holy Trinity.

When God would speak to us in a most appealing way, He moves beyond creation, beyond His omnipotence, His omnipresence, His dominion over all, in all, to the amazing length of the Incarnation in which He sent His Son, the Word, the word of God. God speaks, and His Son is the Word he speaks.

Now, after Ascension, His mission has been accomplished through His life, death, and his rising from the dead. Christ ascends to His Father and promises the ultimate communication, which is the Holy spirit—here all along, but now in a most dynamic, powerful, personal way.

A first fruit of the Spirit's coming is speech. "They spoke in tongues the wonders of God." The Magnalia Dei. And they are commissioned to go forth into all the world and speak the Good News.

Is it not remarkable that our response to all of this is the Silent Life? We are into a cult of quiet, the love of silence, the absence of communication. This gives one pause.

We need not have been in this monastery long to remember restrictions on mail to just a few times a year. And no phones, or with abbreviated dials. Not to mention visits limited to family, if possible, once a year. Here. Not there.

Styles and methods change, but what is current is still a very dramatic art from. There is another communication on another level, in a different strata, in a unique orbit. There is communication with God and with one another and with all the world which is in the grace of God, the life of God, the love of God, by means of which we enter into a communion as real as life and as hidden.

We do not know what life is. We know life only by signs, the signs of life. The inner life of God within is even more subtle, unexplainable. Yet no less real.

When we are in that channel, on that wave length, on that route, we can reach further than any satellite, go as deep as deep can be.

Our silence says this. Glory to God for the marvels the human mind has created in spanning water with magnificent bridges, with mighty tunnels, sending our own kind to the moon and back, project equipment into almost infinite space to listen, to record, to photo—all to the glory of God.

Yet, to reach God is more. To hear God and to worship God is more. Infinitely more. This is the message of the quiet life. Listen! God speaks. He speaks to every human heart. Answer Him, for God awaits a word of love.

Purity of Heart[1]

I was walking down the cloister one day, came by Dom James' office, and on impulse thought I would drop in and let the abbot know how I was doing. I had been here a month or two, a youthful forty-five, fresh from an active mission order, dealing with a change of life. His reception was decidedly cool. I sensed something wrong. Where I came from you could see the rector or the provincial anytime, day or night.

I was told, no matter what you did in the Divine Word society, you don't just drop by the abbot. Certainly not after Prime. There is protocol. You may have done it where you were before, but you can't do it here any more. I was a bit miffed. This man was rather pretentious. Any rector or provincial can do all he does and over far great numbers, and wear no ring, no pectoral cross, carry no crosier, and get no profound bow when you meet. Time changed that when I understood better. You too will never understand that man unless you realize that his love for this abbey was a consuming passion. He was enormously proud of Gethsemani: what it meant, what it stood for. I got the impression that he thought the Catholic Church in America depended on Gethsemani.

It was that love that led him to throw his weight, sometimes gently, sometimes not, on a man he thought would make a good successor as abbot. Why not, pray? Should decades of experience be passed over, the wisdom born of years of service be dismissed? That violated common sense. Why should not an older man counsel a younger? He did this with a pure heart, a good conscience, as they say.

---

[1] This sermon was preached on the occasion of the Silver Jubilee of the election of Abbot Timothy Kelly.

But the monks? Well, they have pure hearts, too. You can be sure they do not stoop to politics, maneuver, power play. That's beneath them. So they did not lean to favored ones. Not on purpose. Maybe not even consciously. Just by instinct, intuitively. They turned their eyes, rather, on a rejected one. Now a few, then more and more. Not because he was the unfavored one—that would be gross—but because in their deeps they wanted one who was his own man. Stand on his own feet. A matter of gut feeling, of the deepest movement of the Spirit. The young abbot at the tiller in rough weather with the old one as his shoulder telling him when to bring the ship around—that was not a picture that appealed at all. The old one should be asleep in his cabin.

But not to spite Dom James, or go counter. No way. It was a deeper matter. At most you can say the former served only as a catalyst. He was the grain of sand that had no business being in the oyster, but was nonetheless cause of the pearl. He was the agent of God's will. That is the fruit of the pure heart, the lesson of the whole business.

The pure of heart are the vessels of God's grace, through which His will is done. Being right or wrong is not the issue. The pure of heart can be mistaken. But God's will can still be done through them. The Cardinals with good heart elected John as a transitional Pope in good faith, and so did the will of God. We know the fruit.

Having a pure heart seems to be the point and purpose of the monastic life. It is thought, of course, that this always leads right to action. But it doesn't; it leads to the will of God, for God can work through the pure. That's why we can love Protestants. We disagree with them theologically, but for the most part, surely, they are pure of heart. God's will would seem to be that we do penance for our sins by suffering divided Christianity.

When the young Canadian with the Basilians took to thinking about being a monk of Gethsemani, the good father and the good mother were not impressed. Not at all. No way. Good people, pure of heart. But, you are not to think the son became a monk to spite them, to show that he could do as he liked. Not at all. That's not the way it is done. Rather, parental opposition was a catalyst that drove the man inward to test his call, to search his heart and confirm his response to grace. The opposition deepened the desire because it questioned it, opposed it. But the response was triggered by the opposition, did not cause it. That would be crude and would never wear anyway.

So when young Kelly crossed the international border, the flag on his father's lighthouse station near Windsor flew at half mast. The mother fumed privately. When he later became abbot, she was more convinced than ever that the whole business was absurd.

You would serve God? Then cultivate the pure heart. Play clean, from the most profound motives. Be barren of pride, of ambition, of self-serving, of play for power, place, position. There is no good in any of that. God cannot operate well in a fouled-up network. The pure of heart can be in error, make mistakes. True enough. No one ever said grace guaranteed success. All we know is that the pure of heart are God's chosen. So we are grateful to Dom James. In ways he was not counting on, he was the agent who perhaps, more than anyone or anything else, began what we celebrate today. We are grateful to him. But our deepest thanks go to Almighty God for what we have received. I hope that the gratitude will encourage us all to foster the pure heart that gives joy to God and brings about His will among us.

His will among us is to do great good. We are prone to identify God's will with tragedy and disaster: fire, earthquake, tornado, famine, plague. We have no other way to cope. But God favors beauty over trial and trouble, yet lacks pure hearts through which to do it. In the pure heart we have the way to blessings, joyous ones. It is no small thing to be agents of such good and to reap the fruit of it too. God prosper the pure heart.

Thank you Father Timothy. It has been a good trip. Good bless you.

A Hopeful Future

The proceedings of the last convention of the American Catholic Theological Society makes excellent light reading before you fall asleep at night. The booklet is not heavy and is easy to hold, but the material is quality.

Here, for example, is the present new generation as described by the experts:

- prone to individualism, relativism, privatism in religion.
- searching for community.
- religiously illiterate, lacking vocabulary or concepts of being a Catholic.
- strong orientation toward voluntary service, but not seen as related to the Church.

If this is our people today, if this is our young people, I daresay there is room for hope.

Privatism, individualism, is very American. We have coped with that for generations, all the way from private interpretation of Scripture to private enterprise in business. Our culture stresses the competitive, the individual. So, that is nothing new.

Quite contrary to that is search for community. That too, remarkably, is very American. From Amish to Hutterites, to Amana, Brook Farm, Quakers, Shakers, Oneida, to New Harmony, community is deep in our psyche.

That we are religiously illiterate is the fruit of public education and Catholic inadequacy. But it is not irremediable. It can be helped. People can learn.

An orientation toward service is beautiful. That it is not identified with the Church is a mark of ignorance and maybe of fear. But it is a great quality.

If you put the whole together, the picture is not grim. A culture of divorce will necessarily result in a generation that trusts nothing, that has no confidence in any structure, not after the love that created you has died, has split. It takes no structure seriously. When the fundamental structure of society—the family—collapses, love for Church or any social or spiritual body will come hard. But it can come; it can be experienced.

The Church is essentially community. And in the Church, how many communities: parochial, diocesan, international, monastic. All kinds. This is our best point, our chief quality.

Let this be known and experienced. If any knew that joy we have in this monastic community—yet, how can you tell anyone. It must be experienced. The desire is there; the hunger is surely a great good.

If we have a generation illiterate in matters of faith, that is not necessarily permanent. Instructing the ignorant is a spiritual work of mercy. We can open doors, share what we have, open our books, invite to choir, welcome at the Eucharist. These are all at once spiritual and educational.

The response to a call to service is surely a reason for hope. The Church is rich in mercy. Its works of charity are phenomenal, but also not well known. The Church is everywhere, even in remote distant lands. Harry Jacobs goes mountain climbing in the Himalayas of Nepal and runs into Sisters of Nazareth from Bardstown. The young go abroad or to the inner city or Andalusia and find the Church already there before them. So if we can make the identification of Christ/-Church/Service, all will come together.

So putting it together, I'd say the situation is encouraging, no matter how discouraging it looks at the moment.

Vocations are not scarce. Vocations are as abundant as ever. It is the response that is weak or lacking or misunderstood.

The power of prayer is great. It has a way of opening eyes, clarifying vision, suggesting options, revealing secrets.

This monastery has been way up and way down. We have been down to thirty and up to two hundred monks or more. They were going to close it once, maybe twice.

Worldwide and in history the scene has been even more chaotic: the Black Death, the Protestant Reformation, the Hundred Years War, the French Revolution, and how many others. Napoleon and Emperor Joseph and the Church itself passed out commendatory abbacies[2] to favorites. Every country in Europe has turned on the church from time to time, and monasteries were easy targets. Yet we Cistercians have been around fo nine hundred years. Not much has been around that long.

So we live in hope. Hope on. Trust God. Pray more. Look to a glorious future. We have been here at Gethsemani for one hundred and fifty years. We're just getting started.

There is a lot of good in the young, even if it is mixed with darkness. That seems to me more or less the way it's always been. Amen.

---

[2]   A commendatory abbot was a distinguished cleric or noble who was made abbot of a monastery by papal or royal decree, without becoming a monk or living in the monastery. He would be custodian of the revenues of the abbey, while the monks were left to the care of the Prior.

The Primacy
of the Spiritual

LUKE 10:1–7

Joseph II, Emperor of the Holy Roman Empire, left his name in history in Josephism, the name given to his gross interference with the running of the Church. He was into everything from sacristy to sanctuary, to seminary to cemetery. His grasp of the Faith was shallow and pathetic. He is especially remembered by the Cistercians, for he is responsible for the split in our Order. He would have no contemplative monks in his kingdom unless they did something practical and useful. In order to survive the monks began schools. They still have them, renowned, of prestige, but they are not really our thing.

We are not practical. We are not useful. We are not into any ministry save hospitality, and that is not ministry as much as courtesy. We are an art form, and as an art form, somewhat exaggerated, as is all art. In order to make a point, let me make an emphatic statement.

What is the statement? The primacy of the spiritual. This monastery makes no sense except spiritually. All we do, all we have, all we are says one thing: there is more to life than what you see. There is more than getting and spending, coming and going. There is a lot more.

We like drama, poetry, song and dance, music. These may have no particular practical value, but are of enormous significance to the human spirit. The world would perish without them. Life would be a desert waste with no poets and dreamers, priests and prophets, monks and mystics.

This is the point that Jesus makes in the Gospel portion this morning. The harvest is rich, so pray for the workers. Spread peace. Carry the word. Spread the news everywhere. Don't worry about equipment and finances, tools and wherewithal. Put first things first; the rest will follow.

No fuss over clothes and food. Carry the good news. Spread it worldwide. If they will not listen, waste no time with them, be gone. There are others waiting to hear you. They will house you, feed you, clothe you, sustain you.

So it has been, is now, ever will be. How many great spiritual enterprises began with no more than an idea and the grace to carry it out? The whole Christian enterprise began with One Person and His twelve disciples. Every religious order began with one person with no resources, no money, no wherewithal. Without exception, the rest all followed. Trust in God and go ahead. The rest will come. Always has. Still does.

The power of the Spirit is enormous and sets into motion great movements of mercy, love, and compassion. Feed the hungry, clothe the naked, shelter the homeless, instruct the ignorant, heal the sick. Wherever Christ goes, wherever the Church goes, the good works follow. They are the concrete expression of this love.

But the first thrust, the main impact, is in the spirit. Christianity is not humanitarianism. If the love of God is not in the good works, they are no more than dole and handout.

Christ often used the emphatic statement to make a point: if your hand offend, cut it off. If your eye would be evil, tear it out. Better one-eyed in Heaven than full vision in Hell. So today: never mind extra sandals, wasting time in casual chatter on the way. No need of a purse full of money, a bag full of clothes. Granted you are sheep among wolves, fear not: I am with you. Preach the word. Drive out demons of doubt and despair. Speak love. Live peace. The rest will follow.

We have been here 150 years. We probably have not made a convert in all that time. No. The conversions follow elsewhere. We sow the seed. We be the witness. We testify to the light. The rest follows. First things first. Seek the Kingdom. The rest will follow.

Hapsburg Joseph is still around in a lot of people without the vision that faith gives. Yet the world itself is testimony to the purpose of a creating God.

God made all for joy, to reveal His glory, to express His delight. We are called to share in it with the same delight, the delight manifest in bug and bird, in lotus and lily, in seeing, hearing, taste and touch. How practical is the rainbow? And if God is so impractical, it is no wonder His works are. We can share His joy, enter it. We can do better than the Hapsburg.

Environmental Impact

MATTHEW 5:1–11
LUKE 6:20–26

People who live by the sea are not too apt to pay a great deal of attention to it, save what is practical and useful: high tide, low tide, a stormy day, a quiet one. The same is true of those who live in the mountains, in a lovely valley, or any locale a visitor would find remarkable for beauty. Such a visitor is likely to think the inhabitants live on a constant high level of awareness of what is around them. Not necessarily so. Sometimes yes, now and then.

Yet on another level, they are continually aware. They never forget. They are always subject to the influence of the lovely around them. The impact of such awareness can be stronger than an occasional conscious attentiveness, or even a persistent one because we are more unconscious than conscious. There is more of one than the other, and we are always being influenced by the greater.

Children of our day can be very violent, not because they are necessarily more violent than those of another day, but because they are submitted to a heavy assault of stimulus to violence from many quarters. We are affected by what we see, what we hear, what we read, by what goes on around us. This is true not only on our conscious level, but even more so on our unconscious level. The darkness of the human psyche is not that difficult to arouse, to stimulate.

Though we perhaps advert little specifically to it, we are as monks submitted to an onslaught of positive, spiritual, beautiful influences. We are profoundly affected by them all. The modest amount of attention that monks give to choir, for example, is not the sum of what choir does to them. The repeated exposure to such power and grace, day after day,

19

night after night, for years on end, has far more influence on the monk than he is aware of, just as his influence on others is once both hidden and enormous.

So we think thoughts of mercy, of pardon, or forgiveness. We live in a climate of love by choice. As Christians we take pains to express this any way we can. The healing of a wound is not the mere application of a dressing and taking a few pills. Every aspect of body and soul, not to say the world around us, is involved. Holistic indeed.

It is good to have trust in all of this. We are truly embraced by the merciful Christ and we live in a country of mercy. It is not imagination or pious fancy. It is not just a pleasant thought, it is reality. Now and then, here and there, we advert to it. Like a stranger coming among us and saying, "What a beautiful place this is." We may almost catch ourselves and respond, "Yes, come to think of it, it is."

The photographer here for the visit of the Dalai Lama was about to board the helicopter back to Lexington when he told the pilot, "Wait a minute. Wait a minute. Let me pull myself together. I have never in my life seen anything as impressive, as beautiful, as what I have just seen. It literally swept me off my feet." And he held his head in his hands.

We live surrounded by such marvelous beauty, and only now and then do we stop to notice it. The healing process never ends.

Years ago monasteries like this were fond of printing sayings of Christ, like the Beatitudes, on the walls of public rooms. Sometimes they were just painted, sometimes, as in Conyers in Georgia, they were cast in cement in the very structure of the chapter room or refectory. No doubt, after some time, no one notices them. Only visitors do. Maybe! Unspoken messages come to us all in many ways, even in what we see and hear day after day. It is good to note the voice of mercy. It is always present.

We are aware enough of the need for a peaceful womb for a child, for excitement, worry, noise, will all affect the growing child in serious ways. We know, too, the beauty of advantaged children brought up in a home of urbanity, good breeding, pleasant surroundings, culture.

So we try in whatever way we can to create a good climate in ourselves, in our inner life of peace, avoiding sin and evil tendencies and cultivating mercy, love, patience, and peace. This can be done in the most discouraging circumstances. It is the point of mercy, of grace. There are people who become beasts in the concentration camp, and people who become saints.

Environment does not create saints, but it sure helps. Not all who emerge from lovely homes are lovely people, and there are wise souls of stature in the slums.

The point remains: in the grace of God we can do far more than we dream possible. It is the basic Christian witness.

Last Mass at Oxford

JOHN 13:31–35

Last Sunday I attended the last Mass at the monastery in Oxford, North Carolina. It was founded thirty years ago by a French Benedictine, Peter Menard, on loan from St. Martin's in Ligugé, France, to be temporary novice master at a new monastery in New York State, Mount Saviour. Finished there, he dreamed of a racially integrated, small foundation. He was much distressed at the state of black Catholics in this country.

He begged funds and built a little plan of a central cottage, several separate cells, a pretty chapel, and a workshop on land belonging to the Diocese of Raleigh. It had an up and down history for a few years, until he developed cancer and had to return to France. He passed it on to some American Benedictines who had it for a while. They gave it to the Cistercians, Gethsemani for three years and then Spencer in 1973 until now. After the Mass there was a picnic under a pavilion which attracted about one hundred friends and neighbors. It was obvious that the place was loved while it lasted.

It did not last. So, do you write it down as a failure? Maybe. What is failure? Not being there at all? Or not staying very long? Is a short life a failure and a long one a success? Do losers never win, do prizes go only to the proficient?

Which brings us to today's Gospel passage. It surely was put in writing only long after Pentecost and after much pondering of the mystery of Christ. For on the face of it Jesus' statement, "now is the Son of Man glorified," is outrageous. It is Holy Thursday night. They have just celebrated the Paschal meal. To it were added some ominous blessings of the bread and the cup, ominous because they spoke of body as broken bread given, of wine offered as blood. Can the disciples have grasped what He meant? And then his talk of glory, he who in a few hours would be prostrate in prayer and sweating blood for the next day. Then betrayed and scourged and crowned in ignominy, passed over in favor of a criminal, dressed immodestly, and led to a hideous death. His followers gone. "Now is the Son of Man glorified." "Bears all the mark of failure," might be a more apt observation.

But we know what follows; the work of God is manifested. Failure becomes triumph. Death makes resurrection possible.

The conclusion is obvious. Human success and human failure, when measured against Christ, are something else again. Grace works in darkness and in light, in failure and success. We never know how or why, or even when.

The only way out of the dilemma is the way of love. His talk of glory was followed by an admonition to love. Love is the key. This is the measure. This is the salvation of the world. Success or failure not. It is a deep lesson for our pondering. Amen.

Thanksgiving Day

 A few months ago a large truck parked overnight on the end of the front avenue. I came out of the chapel, saw the truck and trailer, and asked the man who at the moment came out the retreat house door, "Is that your trailer?"

"Yes, it is."

"And what do you have aboard?"

"Indians."

"And is Massasoit one of them?"

"Yes, he is. I have twelve of them. You have eleven to go."

It turned out that he was a driver and lecturer for a traveling exhibit of twelve historic Indians, life-size mannequins, fully and authentically dressed, set up in large plastic cases. He tours the country: malls, fairs, schools, campuses, announced ahead in the paper, sponsored by the Encyclopedia Britannica. I told him I had been trying for years to get a Britannica here and was always quoted Merton who said, "There had been no real Britannica since the eleventh edition." So, we never got one. "No worry," he said. "I have three sets, 'I'll send you one." And he did. In memory of Massasoit.

It was Massasoit who got the Plymouth pilgrims through the first year and to the harvest feast in celebration of the first Thanksgiving in 1621. They had four turkeys and corn, squash, pumpkins, and cranberries. The custom continues.

Thanksgiving is elemental. Fundamental. The Eucharist is thanksgiving. But the Eucharist, like all prayer, is fourfold: adoration, petition, atonement, thanksgiving. All of these are necessary for complete prayer. That is what makes thanksgiving possible. We are grateful to God for everything.

Once after supper at recreation years ago, I said to gruff, hearty Father Weyland, "It's a lovely day." He growled back at me, "Every day is lovely." I countered, "Surely, some are more loved than others and God must appreciate your noting it."

Yet, for all that, he might be right. All that comes from God is lovely, and we are thankful for all. When Hurricane Hugo was on the way, Mrs. Kline wrote from New Jersey to say, "Thank God it is not headed here, but further south." Next day she wrote again, "What a terrible thing to say. I did not mean it."

Was Abbot Francis Kline in South Carolina grateful for Hugo? Was anyone? I daresay most people take what comes from God and waste no time complaining, but get busy cleaning up the mess.

It is good to follow the old pious phrase about the "adorable will of God," and unite the adoration of God to accepting His Holy Will, whatever it be. The AA prayer says it perfectly: "God grant me the serenity to accept the things I cannot change, courage to change the things I can, and wisdom to know the difference."

Accepting the will of God is not passive. That is why uniting it to petition and atonement is so sound. We cannot use the will of God as a cover for helplessness. We cannot sink into self-pitying misery as the will of God. This is the fruit of anger and resentment. We ask God's help, we acknowledge that as sinners we have a guilt that has made the world a communal experience of penance.

There is a kind of docility that is much a part of our life in God. There seems to be a time in God's plan that we may not take to.

When I was eighteen, I entered a seminary, a minor seminary actually, for I lacked Latin and Greek. It was of a missionary order. I really was looking for monastic life, did not know it, and was not aware that there were monasteries. Twelve years of public school exposed me to the medieval church, but not to much of the contemporary scene. I was thus drawn to an order, missionary or not, rather than to the diocese. Later on, when I was better informed, I told the Fathers of my monastic interest. They discourage me as a most unlikely prospect for the monastic life. I accepted that. Later on, in college years, I mention the matter to my director and was told that such a life was not suited to me. Very well. Once a novice, then in vows, I laid aside any monastic fantasies as disloyal and a lack of commitment.

But now and then I would be haunted. One of the workers at the Seminary joined the monastery in Rhode Island. Later, one of the Divine Word fathers joined Gethsemani, but a few years later returned when war made any Philippine foundation impossible, his dream and the abbot's. But I was much troubled.

The years went by and nothing ever came of a youthful dream. Then, some years later, a combination of items—a disastrous fire in which I was almost caught, a change in policy with the magazine I edited, and I was adrift in mid-term. No specific obligations for this brief moment—rare in religion, or anywhere else for that matter—and I thought, here is your chance. It will never come again, not when you are forty-five.

So, I came here, I looked, I liked, I asked. I was released from the Divine Word Society and admitted to the Cistercians with small enthusiasms on either side. I did not care. It turned out to by a rough road, but the right one, in 1960.

The point is, things have their time. One is not to force, to insist. As it turned out, my action background and training, my mission exposure and experience, my community life for twenty-five years, all were great assets.

If God wills it, it will come. Patience is prayer, too.

We adore God. We thank God, and we thank Him for everything. We petition our God because we have needs. We need Him to lead us not into temptation, but deliver us from evil. We acknowledge we are sinners who deserve far more than the crucifixion Jesus got, and so take what comes and get going.

Dorothy Day saw as much of the seamy side of life as many and far more than most. She asked for two words on her tombstone: Deo Gratias. Thanks be to God. God sent Massasoit to the pilgrims in desperate need and a Britannica to those who could use it. He is not beyond helping us, for thanksgiving is graceful.

All Saints Day

Some centuries down the times to come I envision Cistercian monks coming from, say, Malaysia, to probe the ruins of Gethsemani Abbey. These would-be archeologists would have known that this continent was devastated by some nuclear disaster, seemingly accidental, centuries earlier, and was therefore until now wholly inaccessible. Now it was safe. And though they knew there were several abbeys in the land, Gethsemani was the first, best known, and best documented. They wanted to see if they could find the saint's grave. They eventually located the place by following the dry bed of the Ohio river and learned much, confirmed much.

They ran into problems, however, when they discovered the sealed cave in the cliff at the edge of the bottom, and could not account for it. One knowledgeable monk who had read the ancient literature declared it was a bomb shelter, not, as they first supposed, a cheese cellar. In fact, he said, some of the monks were displeased with it and said they would not use it with other people in the area helpless. The abbot told them in reply, so the story goes, that it was fully justified because, "the church needs us."

One of the spiritually astute among them declared that the abbot of old was right, the church did need them.

Such a fantasy, while admittedly unlikely to take place, is, as you know well enough, also admittedly very possible. If the thought gives rise to considerations fitting the end of the year and the end of all things, it also helps us in our response to All Saints.

Is there any significance for the world or the church in a group dedicating itself to a life of prayer, to singing Psalms, to offering the sacrifice of the Mass, and pursuing the quiet life? One would think so.

The Church does not exist without Christians, for that is what the

Church is. Christ is indeed present on the earth, even in the earth, as the cosmic Lord of history, but His place of privilege is in the hearts of the people. Without them, He is not here as Redeemer. Without them His work of redemption is not accomplished.

A group of monks is not the church nor the Christian world. Rather, they are a significant expression of the Church and the Christian life and, as significant, signify the whole. We can speak of the Church in this context as the Mystical Body of Christ, of all who love God as they can. It is through them with Christ that the world is redeemed. A monastery, the monastery of Gethsemani, is significant because every Christian, everyone who loves God, is significant. Through them all, Christ saves all, please God.

When we ponder this truth we perhaps reach the ultimate expansion of the call of our believing. To accept the annunciation, the birth, the life of teaching and healing, the passion, death and rising of Jesus, His sending of the Spirit, the founding of the Church, all as objects of our faith can be managed with the grace of God without great difficulty. They are all of them historic events with named people in known places. But when we move on to the mystical presence of God on earth we begin to touch something quite beyond our grasp.

There are literally billions now on earth with us. How many of them are Catholic? We can at least estimate. How many know God, love Him, serve Him, we have no way of knowing. And how many in ways subtle and ill-defined truly seek Him is far beyond our ken. We are dealing with astronomic numbers even when considering merely our contemporaries here on earth. We cannot cope with the numbers here before us and now gone into eternity, or those yet to come. They all live, and hopefully, all live with God through Christ and are united with Him. Or will one day.

There is no notion that so taxes our mind for sheer magnitude of scope. We believe, in the grace of God, that our union with Christ has meaning for all who live and are united with us in grace for the Kingdom.

Though I do not suggest that we ought to strain our imagination in trying to objectify all this, I do feel in some way that we ought to be conscious of it. We tend inevitably to underestimate our role a Christians, let alone as monks, not just because we have a modest view of ourselves and should not be pretentious, but because we do not reckon that the one we love and serve is Jesus Christ, Son of God Almighty, redeemer of the world, savior of all.

Joy, then, is the first sequel to these notions, the first derivative. What greater joy could there be than to participate in some drama of eternal meaning for all who live? We do so in faith. That faith is made articulate by vow, by virtue, by good word, good deed, by the consecrated life of service, by where we live, by what we wear, what we eat and what we do all day and why.

"Eye has not seen," nor do we expect to, and "ear has not heard," nor do we count on it to do so, nor has it entered the human mind to conceive "what God has prepared for those who love Him," and for those whom they love. It is all in faith. Without that faith we are still in darkness and sin and the whole world absurd and meaningless, sick with violence and hate. With that gift we accomplish in Christ salvation in this world and the world to come. Amen.

Come and See

 ## JOHN 1:35–42

The Gospel today is on the call and first response to the call. As happens so often, it begins with a question and a wrong answer. The two disciples followed Jesus when He was pointed out as the "Lamb of God" by John the Baptist. Jesus saw them following him and so asked, "What are you looking for?" They did not answer, but instead asked another question, "Rabbi, where do you stay?" To which he responded with an invitation, "Come and see." It was an exchange of enormous significance, and they never forgot it. The remembered even the time of day it took place. "It was about four in the afternoon."

Most people who are called have a sense of some important desire which is lost in memory. But they can tell you easily enough the time and place they first acted on it. The matter used to be called vocation. In years past a great stress was placed on whether or not one had this impulse born of God, this inner spiritual awareness of being summoned to God's service. The discernment of the qualities of this call, how it was to be interpreted, how intense an experience it was, grew very complex. At times it outweighed what other qualities might be assumed more or less essential in a call, in favor of the call itself. In the end, an overwrought concern settled for the actual call of the bishop to ordination or of the superior to vows, to be the vocation. Anything less than that was preliminary, was preparation, offering.

Today, with few offerings being made to bishops or superiors, the discussion seems a bit academic. Yes the question does arise, is God still calling?

Are we to assume that no candidates or few means no vocations, or few? Does God withhold His favors on occasion? What are we to make of the fact that despite the need for workers, we see little response? My feeling, perhaps yours, is that the call goes out, but they are few who answer.

A culture needs men of God, women of God. A Catholic culture needs priests, brothers, sisters, monks, and nuns. A culture, Catholic or not, needs poets, writers, dramatists, dancers, prophets, actors, singers. What if they are not forthcoming or in short supply? I suppose one could issue a great deal of promotional literature, make facilities for training available, reward excellence with recognition and honors. All with help. You could import from overseas to stimulate the local appetite and emulation. Yet, it is clear from the outset that such artists are in good supply when they are appreciated and recognized. No writer, singer, actor, musician, could survive without recognition.

It is just possible that our people no longer appreciate what they have in the church and its servants. If there are observable trends in average Catholic lives which are at odds with serious Catholic teaching, it is not too difficult to assume that a certain disenchantment will color a response to the local Father. Such a response need never be vocal or explicit to have power and influence. The young will read it with ease: the service of God does not rate a high priority.

This not to say that styles do not change. They do, and people change with styles. The Catholic laity are no longer immigrants or first generation. They have moved up on the social scale as all good Americans do. They are not only—many of them—well educated, but better educated than many clerics. Though sisters as a group are a well educated body of women, well educated women are far more numerous today. So the approach of nuns is somewhat different, more mature, perhaps, less subservient.

The Father is different too. He prefers not to take privilege for granted from police, clerical discount for all his purchases, a tip of the hat from the passersby, better transport, housing, attire than the average. All these went out with the biretta. They are not in vogue. Moreover, the role is cast in a new mode. The priest today is spiritual master, director of souls, part of a team of competent experts in the matters of the spirit. More good preaching is essential, not exceptional. He will be admired not for building or fundraising, which others can do, but for good liturgy and for social concern. So the casting is for a new kind of man, and he emerges in response to need, to demand.

What makes for poets is people who read poetry. Musicians thrive when people like music. Artists flourish where art is appreciated. Songs are written and are sung to people who want to hear them and sing them. Priests abound when there are people who want them, love them, need them, and know it.

The burden on priests is enormous, for not only do they move into new modes, but often have to face the diffident or the hostile who have an argument with God, a bone to pick with God's church.

For all that, great things go on and great good is done. If you wring your hands, spare yourself. There is a spiritual ferment in our midst and it is of gigantic proportions. We need to move into affirmation for priest and altar, love for the word of God and the one who preaches it, love for superb liturgy and sacred art and good music and social concerns. This is a favorable climate for priests.

When Dom James years ago in the late 1950s came to the conviction that there would be no stopping a new world movement for a liturgy in one's own language, he moved effectively. Early on, in Advent, 1960, he introduced the lay brothers to an English office. In one act he prepared the brothers who would want to join the monk's choir and at the same time gave occasion to experiment by a living model that was certain to come, an English liturgy. He had no doubt of it and was right.

He could not have been surprised when monks were not interested in the Pope's plea to keep the old Latin liturgy in monasteries. Keeping alive an antiquity had no appeal. So the ground was plowed and harrowed in view of what was to come. There was a receptive, welcoming climate that made a nine hundred year old heritage something whose time had some, whose noble service was over.

It is the supportive climate that makes flowers bloom and artists grow. I suppose that if there are not enough priests, it is that they are not wanted badly enough. There is not enough love for them.

We have always had a few monks whose families did not think highly of their calling, but by and large we are loved. We are a breed who needs love. And who does not?

Jesus' call, then, in the gospel is weighted. It is a personal call to the individual—"from now on you shall be called Peter"—but it is a call also to the whole body who will support him in his call. The very love of the servant becomes the very love of his Master who called him.

Change

For the past ten years or so I have been offering Mass each day after Vigils in the chapel. With the Roman Canon, and sung, according to the music printed at the rear of the Missal. You'd think, wouldn't you, that others might take up the practice—not of a daily Roman Canon, or after Vigils, but sung? Granted that we do not have an abundance of priests, some of them can sing at least as well as I do. No takers. Why? One could take it personally and say, "Well, no one takes up any idea I suggest." But that would be silly. And incorrect. It's more a generic thing, characteristic of communities, especially religious communities. They tend to be conservative, are traditionally oriented, don't relish change. Least of all being trendy.

When Brother Roger was last here, he told me that he was working the while for his brother, a sign-maker. "Ah!" I said. "That's great. I wonder if he works with neon." "Yes, he works with neon." "Fine. I have an idea. I'd like a large cross in blue neon on the water tower on the hill. You know, it looks like a mighty Easter candle. We could Easter-candle it and mount a long strip of blue neon up and down, and a strip across for a cross. And the year 2000 at the center. Maybe an Alpha and Omega at the end of the cross arms. Could he do that?" "sure, he could do that. No problem." "For the millennium, you know. So people going by wouldn't think the place some school or state prison. How much, do you think?" "Oh, a couple of thousand." So I submitted it to the council. It didn't even make the minutes. So, it's personal? They don't take up any suggestion I offer? No, not at all. It's generic. They don't cotton to new ideas. They resist innovations. It's characteristic.

Christ's encounter this morning at Capernaum is revealing. A group had gathered in the house where He was staying. He was giving them the good news He came to proclaim when they brought a young paralytic to Him, hoping He would heal him. But they couldn't get close enough to ask Him. So they climbed up on the roof, removed the tiles and lowered the paralytic to a place close to His feet. Christ would have been somewhat amazed, or more likely amused, at their determination. He looked with affection on the youth and told him to "be of good heart, for I forgive you your sins."

The scribes prominent in the gathering reacted in character, distressed at this unheard of presumption. They raised their eyebrows, gave each other knowing looks. They pursed their lips and nodded knowingly. Christ need not have read their minds. He had only to look at their faces. "The man blasphemes! Who can forgive sin but God alone?" Their generic reactions blinded them to the obvious. If only God can forgive, maybe He is God. "Which is easier: to heal or to forgive?" "Get up. And go home," He said to the youth. High drama in a low room packed with a delighted audience who rubbed it into the traditionalists: "We've never seen anything like this, have we now?"

We are going to be electing a new abbot for this house in a month or two. It surely cannot be out of place to suggest that some concern over our own generic tendency to stick to what we are used to will need some deft handling.

Hopefully, we shall elect an abbot even better than the one we had. We stiffen that hope with prayer. That hope being somewhat unrealistic, we pray that at least we get one as good as what we've had.

Yet, one thing is certain. Whether he is better than what we had or as good or far worse, he will assuredly be different. And his being different will require some openness, some give in your stance, some limber in your muscle if you are going to survive. Your commitment is going to have to go deeper than a mere comfortable content with what you are used to, to a deep submission to God's will revealed in His providence.

Which, after all, is an application of our faith common to all. Conformity to God's will is the key to happiness. Any generic inertia that resists change can lead us far astray, as it led the scribes to what is to be avoided at any cost. Better bend than break, better keep flowing rather than freeze. No skyscraper ever broke in the wind: they bend. No vowed life ever lasted without supple love. Amen.

2 ~ Issues of Faith

Ash Wednesday

As the end approached, and Father Vianney realized it, he did a very monk thing. He got out of bed, got into his habit, wandered around the monastery a bit for the last time, returned to his room, lay prostrate on the floor, face down, *modo monastico*, that is, his hands flat and his forehead lying upon them, and so waited for the Lord, Who came and got him. On the floor—symbol of the earth from which he came: *mater*, mother, matter. Dust, ashes.

Primitive people opted to be born literally on the earth, and to die, literally, on the earth. Father Vianney was witness, in the vivid style he loved, to the human condition. Some ashes smeared on your forehead will deliver you the same message this morning.

Ash Wednesday, among other things, is an admission and an acceptance of the human condition. If "dust to dust" was not spoken to the soul, it is still in the dynamics of human existence, something we deal with for the reason that life will end—in ashes.

We come face to face with the consequences in our endeavors to know God. Nowhere else do our limits make themselves so prominent. Already in early centuries the matter of our knowing God fascinated brilliant minds and led to developments that set patters that have come down to us.

In speaking of God, we move in three fields: affirmation, negation, expansion.

We note a good in our existence. We *affirm* that it is from God. Then we *deny* all that limits the affirmed good. And finally, we *expand* it infinitely to apply it to God.

We note goodness. We think of God as good and apply it to Him. Before doing so, we strip goodness of its human limitations, and then apply it to God in a most eminent way. And so we come to the knowledge of God by analogy. What other way is there? "If you, evil as you are, know how to give good things to your children, how much more your heavenly Father!" Jesus taught us by analogy.

Our talk of God, then, is not *univocal*, for human good and divine good are not the same. Nor is our talk *equivocal*, that is, almost meaningless for being applied so disparately. But there is enough in common with human good and divine good to see something that is in both.

It is by analogy that we know God. He is like this, He is like that. This basis on which this rests is that it is God who has revealed Himself in all creation. "The world is charged with the grandeur of God" (Hopkins). We can read Him in creation, by *analogy*, by *causation*. We use *metaphor*: God is a rock, a firm foundation. We use *relationship*: God is Redeemer, my Savior. We use *negation*: God is without limit. He has no end, no beginning, no height, no depth. God is infinite.

Yet, in all analogy, in all use of metaphor, relationship, negation, we know our limits, for we cannot ascribe the merely human to God in any adequacy. All analogy breaks down.

We reveal this unknowability of God in giving Him many names. How many the images, the likenesses of God! If we knew God we would give Him a name, but we do not and cannot and so He has many names, each revealing a little, the total of them far from reality.

Vatican I put it so: "Divine mysteries of their very nature so excel the created intellect that even when they have been given in revelation and accepted in faith, that very faith still keeps them veiled in a sort of obscurity as long as we are exiled from the Lord in this mortal life."

"If you understood," so Saint Augustine, "then this is not God. If you were able to understand, then you understand something else instead of God. If you were able to understand even partially, then you have deceived yourself with your own thoughts."

This God, so inadequately known through human knowledge, concepts, intellectualizing, is know truly only through love, for God is love. We know Go not in the mind, in words and concepts, but in the heart, in love.

Our human condition places us before a God who is inconceivable, immortal, invisible, infinite, and so beyond our grasp as to lead us to despair. "In loving we already possess God as known better than we know our fellow human whom we love. Much better, in fact, because God is nearer, more present, more certain," wrote Saint Augustine.

"I am who am," the "One who is," was God's name as given to Moses in the burning bush. Here ultimately being is called God—the first, the original, the only real being, for all other being is derived, and all that is can only be in God's sharing the capacity to be. Yet when we say He is "Being," we have not come near the truth for the reason that we cannot. In the end we fall to our knees in awe before ineffable mystery, and we give love to Love for we cannot help but do so and know His love in our very being.

We note the wind—the gentleness of God in a light breeze off the sea, the power of God in a mighty wind, the wisdom of God in the clouds that bring rain, the wind-borne seeds that support birds, prosper growth, supply trees. We stand in the rain that can by turn be dew, be fog and mist and frost, be snow and hail and ice and rainbow, and we wonder about the God who enjoys them so. We walk the beach to watch the surf and recall the quiet days when it is wincing glass, storm days when tons of water come crashing on the coast. There is no end of God manifest above us, around us, beneath us, within us. God beyond us utterly. Utterly.

Ashes indeed reveal the glory of God that fills the world. Amen

Manifestations
of God

God created the universe, this world, and having created it sustains it. As the Spirit hovered over the primal chaos, so He continues to be present in all that is. "The world is charged with the grandeur of God," said the poet, and the charge is His presence, His providence, His guidance.

Yet, in terms of His relation to the human, God was subject to diffidence, hostility, malice, and ignorance. He cannot, will not, does not over-ride human freedom, and hence is rendered powerless to one degree or another.

Yet, God is manifest in culture, in religious endeavor, in learning, in art, in science, in all of human industry and prowess, in human love and human desire. What is glibly called "nature" or even "mother nature," is, of course, ultimately God. His first endeavor to enter, however carefully, into deeper relations with us was with Israel, and what a stormy, difficult relation it was. But in the end God prevailed and the dream unfolded, and God became man, one of us, a human. There were tragic consequences which love and mercy overcame.

This sublime Christian story exploded into unbelievable reality in the coming of the Holy Spirit on this Pentecost, fifty days after Easter, ten days after the Ascension. History is now forever changed. God's presence among us is of a new order, another dimension, quiet unlike anything before: His creative, providential omnipresence. Now He engages with the human freed of the blindness of sin, the tyranny of evil and darkness. As long as we live in His grace, we live in His power and love as a holy priesthood, a holy people of God. Grace and light began in Jerusalem and spread thence for all time over all the world, a new creation in the Spirit.

We ought not to take our priesthood lightly, this holy people of God, nor be reluctant, diffident, aloof, unresponsive to grace. We are called to praise, to honor, to glorify God as this holy people of God, anointed and consecrated to His service. His ordained priest is but an articulate expression of this whole. As a priestly people we are to make God explicit in all of life.

Looking back, it is not difficult to trace divine design. We see His handiwork revealed in the brilliance of the human mind, the potential of the human for beauty, love, wisdom, growth in all the arts. All is inspired by the Spirit who is able to do so much when the human is freed of sin and enlightened by grace.

Human progress through the centuries is a marvel to consider and one does not consider it right unless in the light of God. Yet, we still know sin, often in darkness. We betray light and repudiate good. Evil sweeps through the world, but the light is still there, and the good. They will not perish. God abides in His Church until the end of time.

Vision is the gift of looking forward and dreaming of a better world, but wisdom comes from looking back and considering, and so to learn. Wisdom is more characteristic of the old than of the young. The young look forward, the old look back, and looking back has its rewards. Since all theology is personal, it is natural to trace one's own life's track and the marvel of God's design, His providence, His care, His love.

One is aghast at how dangerous it was, what risks were taken, what boldness, how causal the browsing with evil. How splendid the kind mercy of God Who managed to turn all to good.

That is why a man sixty years a priest, as one of our monks is today, does not look back, as it were, with pride and satisfaction at a job well done. No way. It is rather the bewildering realization that it was all gift, all love from God. We thought all along—as the young will do—that we had it all in hand, could take care of things, would manage, for the love of God, of course. Alas, alack! How naïve. How simple-minded.

Hence, thanks, gratitude, from our heart to His heart. Thank you very much for all that God poured into our world in such munificence. We are grateful for all, and, at the same time, repentant that we have bungled so much and still do, out of ignorance, malice, stupidity, and pride. We beg pardon. *Lava quod est sordidum. Riga quod est aridum. Sana quod est saucium.* Wash filth, send rain, heal wounds. Amen.

On to a Good Thing

John 20:19–23

You have a good product,
    let us say a very good product,
    a first class fruit cake or a cheese,
    it is not enough to assume that excellent quality
    will sell it.
You cannot wrap it in newspaper.
It is going to take tasty packaging,
  apt advertising, too.
We know, this is our business.
You know it as something obvious to a consumer as much as
  to a producer.

A certain élan must surround creation if its true value is to be appreciated.

Everything that God has created has this aura, most of all his superb creation, humankind. Not to be aware of this is to live the deprived life.

We are immortal. That is to say, our death is a transition to a higher life. It is not an end. This fact of our immortality cannot be hidden. It keeps manifesting its reality, a secret no one can keep.

It would seem that one effect of sin, both personal and general, is a certain shame about our kind, and a doubt that we are as special as some would have us believe. It is not that we have cone down from a high station, but that we never had one.

All the same, people from one end of the world to the other, in this era and every other, deny what they say by what they do. What they do makes clear that they believe they are gods, immortals, even if, and especially if, they are not even aware that they do so.

Else why do people gather wealth, practice kindness, seek happiness, cultivate art, play music, stage drama, dance for joy, climb mountains, swim in the sea, seek wisdom, write books, celebrate anniversaries, note birth and death, wedding and graduation, build homes with hearths, families with love, and work, work, work? You cannot be naïve enough to pretend that none of this is tied to eternity! Surely! For they bear pain, too.

One grace of our Christian faith is that it frees us from that dreadful need to apologize for being what we are. It frees us from that compulsion to dress in rags a royal line, to be tirelessly poor-mouthing ourselves who are to inherit the riches of the kingdom, who curse ourselves for being loved. These are the works of darkness. We can leave them behind. There is no need to beg pardon for being alive, nor is there humility in claiming that we do not matter.

An aura surrounds us as bright as blinding light. Only they who choose not to, do not see it. And even so, this is but the enhancement of what God Almighty has made. If even that dazzles us, what is to be said of the ultimate revelation?

So bless yourselves, good Christian people, with the sign of the trinity, the holy cross, in the morning when you rise from sleep, and at night when you return to it. Going and coming, eating and drinking, working and playing, you have no idea who you really are.

But if you and I in faith have but an inkling of it, we are onto a good thing, and it sure beats walking in darkness.

A Call Universal
and Unique

LUKE 13:22–30

> "I am coming to gather all nations and tongues; and they shall come and see my glory. To the coastlands far away that have not heard of my fame or seen my glory; and they shall declare my glory among all the nations. They shall bring all your kindred from all the nations as an offering to the Lord... to my holy mountain Jerusalem." (from Isaiah 66)

That is the most explicit statement in the Old Testament of both Yahweh's universal claim and the particularity of Jerusalem. It is a foretelling, an eschatological discourse, of the universal call to salvation in the unique God and His unique Church. It is good, it is refreshing, to grasp the simplicity of it, the bold thrust of it: there is one God, one Lord, one faith, one baptism, for all.

And yet in the Gospel passage it is made clear that though the call is universal and unique, the door is narrow and the passage to life is difficult. People will come from east and west, from the north and the south, and will take their places at his feast. Some will not make it. "I do not know you, nor where you come from." Here indeed must be a reconciliation of opposites, and that, of course, is not unusual in Christianity.

The words of Christ make it clear: a universal call, but the gate is narrow. There is a summons to unity in God, and yet some are excluded. Narrow the gate and hard the way that leads to life.

There is this uncomfortable note in Christianity that expects us to make great leaps of faith. We must manage somehow in nature and grace to use both hands to grasp a reality that is seemingly contradictory and too much to manage. That is what constitutes the rough road and the narrow door.

One thinks of that when one thinks of the Irish. Surely they are a people beloved of God, surely a people blessed with kinship to the world of the spirit, a people of the wind and the rain and the sea, of remote islands, dynamically communal and passionately solitary. They are great fighters, great poets, gifted in speech, in human encounter, in humor.

If they have been so blessed, then why so cursed? Why are they so misery-ridden. The English are Teutonic and the Irish Celt. They do not meet. They live in different worlds. They do not understand one another. Good enough: people differ. But the Irish were miserably oppressed by the British for seven centuries. More than that, oppressed because they were Catholic. The Irish never had a colony because they never were a country, never oppressed another people because they were never there to oppress.

To this people dearly beloved by God and so heavily burdened, a sweet Providence sent, one hundred fifty years ago in 1845, a five year famine that left at least one million dead and drove abroad two million more. So what have we done to deserve this? One does not speak so, even when famine was followed by the severest winter in history with mild westerlies replaced by snow-bearing gales from the plains of Russia that brought six inches of snow to Ireland.

Instead of complaint, look around. There are millions of Irish all over the world, and where the Irish went, the faith went. They brought their gifts and graces to many lands. This was the fruit of starvation and tyranny. In the eighteenth, nineteenth, and twentieth centuries, seven million Irish came to this country alone. Their descendants are some 40 million today.

Is this good? Is this God's work? Is this sweet Providence? One would think so. It is a marvel, is it not? To be sure, not all that unique, for there are other peoples who knew oppression and other migrants also richly gifted and highly endowed. But the Irish are a good sample.

The lesson is clear. Bear what must be borne for Christ's sake, in the hope that somehow, somewhere, sometime, great good will come of it.

This is not Irish superstition, it is the Faith. It is to reconcile peace and joy with suffering and death. The road is rough and the gate narrow, and I don't think it can be other than that, can it?

The call is universal—extended to all, and it is a call to unity in the

one God in Christ. To maintain such a faith is witness to the significance of human existence. What we do here is prologue, is prelude and
overture to the ultimate reality in the life of come.

The Portuguese left Goa in India. We left Manila in the
Philippines. The English have left Hong Kong, and Ireland, too.
Oppression and subjugation are not it. Not it at all. The gift we carry
and leave behind is the Faith, and that is from God, by any of us, by way
of suffering and death, famine and cold win from Russia.

Indifferent Sickness

 ## Matthew 16:13-19

We are so used to extraordinary complexity that we make little of it: the gifts of sight, sound, and speech, for example; memory and imagination, color and feeling. What of the complexity behind this gathering, the intricate network of circumstances and trifles that has brought us together into one house and community? It is a marvel of God, surely a superb combination of human desire and divine design.

Did Peter just happen? And Paul? Was it fate, luck, chance, or destiny that threw them together in the world's greatest enterprise? Or was it the fruit of God's maneuvering?

It is healthy sometimes to face the mysteries of our lives. As Christians we are willing and able to sense the providence of God in life, and yet doing as much does not take us very far. We still do not know how real we are and how real God is. It is to deal with what we call mystery in the classic sense, that is, truth beyond our comprehension, our full understanding. The mystery of Peter and Paul is no greater than our own.

What we really ought to understand is now great is our need for mysteries and the pondering of them. We are immortal. A simple enough statement, but a truth almost incomprehensible, yet it is basic, elemental to any grasp of human existence.

To stand in awe before unassailable truth is nurturing, is extremely healthy and health promoting. Likewise, to live indifferently to the mystical leads inevitably to sickness. The flight from the world of faith is disastrous.

Hence, to look on Peter and Paul in some honesty is to tune in to the play of God in human history. Peter was an unlikely prospect for any serious endeavor: charming, generous, enthusiastic, but unsteady, fickle, and cowardly. To him were entrusted the keys. Paul was a proud bigot, self-righteous, vindictive, and prone to posturing. Yet he was chosen to be the apostle to the Gentiles. With such material the power of God made heroes. They were the very human foundation of a very human Church which is at once the presence and power of Christ on earth.

If all you see is present reality, you do not see at all. If you are blind to the mystical dimension of the human scene, you might as well be physically blind for all the good it does you. We need and are nourished by the depths of faith. This feast of Peter and Paul is a call to that.

Our liturgy this morning speaks of this. We had a Byzantine liturgy and Mass, the rite of St. John Chrysostom, by a great priest and choir. If our worship deals in special clothes, rites, and ceremonial, in candle and cup, wine and bows—all in a special place by special people for a special reason—so today's liturgy is doing as much more emphatically for being unfamiliar and strange. All of this is to break the bondage of the banal and commonplace, to open us to the world of God and spirit.

We all have hidden dimensions more real than the obvious and visible. Our very being here is witness to that. Peter and Paul are two ordinary men caught up in a net of God's providence to be involved in the most sublime engagement on earth—the Kingdom of God. Peter and Paul and what they were about will mean little to you unless you are open to the God active in your own human life. You are caught up in a glorious business that Peter and Paul knew. The stakes are no less. The rewards are real. Amen.

Probing the Depths

Luke 20:27–38

Sail into deep waters and you do not run aground. In the deep waters take frequent soundings and you will fare well.

Deep waters are favored by the faithful. We thrive on mystery, on the incomprehensible and the outrageous. No one claims or can claim that our faith violates reason, but no one denies either that it passes beyond reason into realms of another kind. The realms of faith are deep, and we need them far more than any mariner.

We talk easily of immortal life, of life forever with God, of profundities we grasp only in a very modest way. Yet the probing and the pondering do not just fascinate; they nurture our being. We are immortal, and immortality is nourished by deep mystery. Echoes resound through our souls when we are exposed to heavenly music.

In the reading from Luke the Sadducees pose a problem that they were sure had no answer. They had no answer and were just as certain that Christ could not provide one. One woman was married to seven husbands in succession. Whose wife is she in the life to come?

"She does not have a husband in the life to come," is His answer. "They do not marry in Heaven. They are like the angels."

In just a handful of words He ruined their case. We are not husbands and wives in Heaven, nor singles, virgins, divorced, divorced and remarried, widows, widowers. Life on earth is not like life in Heaven, for in Heaven there is no death. It is eternal. The whole, the integral, the complete lack nothing, want nothing, never die.

All of which we understand. We know the meaning of the words, but as far as grasping the significance of what we talk about, we are at a loss.

Yet we need to return to such deeps and probe them. Doing so enhances and enriches life. We deal with verities, with mystery to be sure, the incomprehensible, but with the real and the true.

"They are like angels." In what way? In having no bodies? No. Being pure spirit? No. What then? It is a matter of wholeness of being, fullness of person.

Now on earth we build koinonia, we create community, family, brotherhood. In the Kingdom we need no longer build so. In wholeness we do not need one another. The love we have for one another will move from mutual need to mutual wholeness.

In that wholeness of being we embrace all being in God. The faith that we have in the Kingdom to come now already gives glory to God, gives Him praise. More than that, it gives glory to life and praises it.

For our entering into the world of faith is no escape into delusion and fantasy. It is no abandonment of responsibility. Just the opposite. It is a plunge into the deeps that sustain us.

We are constantly tempted by the Evil One to deny our significance and take comfort in a shallow life, a life without depth.

Thus our faith, far from being some cowardly escape, is a plunge into profound reality that will come home to us in shattering fulfillment beyond our wildest dreams.

No baby in the womb can have but the slimmest notion of what lies beyond the enclosure of its little world. However painful is the leaving of it, it is the only way to life. It is fulfillment.

So our faith—however absurd it may seem to those who do not venture in deeps—gives the sort of meaning and purpose to existence that resounds in our depths and gives a meaning and significance to that existence that absolutely nothing on earth can shake, or weaken, or destroy. In the midst of whatever comes, it is pure joy.

Mystical Time

 ## MATTHEW 28:1–10

Forty-five years ago, in February, 1951, Pope Pius XII began the renewal of Holy Week when he moved the Easter Vigil to the evening. He added a prayer to the ancient rite which can be a key to an understanding of the mysteries of Christ's passion, death, and rising, "Christ yesterday and today, the beginning and the end, Alpha and Omega. All time belongs to Him and all the ages. To Him be glory and power through every age forever."

The text is a key because it highlights the role of time in our celebration. Tonight we do not merely hold a memorial service. Rather, we move out of experienced time into mystical time, God's now, grace time. We do not simply hear the Passion sung, recall His dying, and recount His rising. We are instead present. These all happen now because liturgically we are not in literal time. The implications are breath-taking.

There is a sense of this when Louisville people are told that their parish church will be closed, perhaps sold, even torn down. It is more than mere memory or sentiment, a life-long association. It is rather that religion and the service of God touch eternity. A place that has known commerce with the eternal is too holy to be closed, to be sold, to be torn down. This insight in some way may color their reaction to a situation.

The Church shares this view in retaining the names of dioceses long since gone, gone even physically. Bishops who do not function as Ordinaries are made titular bishops. In a way, a diocese goes on, no matter what the actual situation may be. Something holy is forever holy.

In France, a diocesan bishop who fell out of favor was moved and made titular bishop of Partenia, a place long since burned in the sands of

Algeria. A friend on the internet created a web page for Partenia. By it, the bishop is in instant contact with uncounted numbers who can reach him at any moment from anywhere in the world. He is the world's first internet bishop. The diocese lives on by virtue of electronic communion.

In the grace of God in the holy mysteries of these days of the Great Week, the curtain parts, torn from top to bottom, and reveals a glimpse of timeless eternity, the eternal now of God. This is wholly incomprehensible to us and yet far more real than the construct we call time that we live in, let alone some computer world.

Here is more than intimation of immortality. The life we know is not mere human life; it shares the divine. The passion, death and rising are no mere memories, but actualities we witness, share in, are part of.

This gives life a scope almost unbelievable. It makes Christ's passion personal, for we have a hand in it as sinners. We witness a hideous death undergone for us. We witness under our Paschal moon a glorious rising on the first day of a new time.

All of this is a bit much for frail human nature. Hence, we experience it in touches, hints and moments of light, but for real.

We venerate old ruins. We treasure relics of the past. We keep alive memories of great ones gone, not to bring back the past, or that we not forget, but to suggest that there is more than time. We believe that, know that, for it is the Christ of yesterday and today, the beginning and the end, the Alpha and Omega. All time and all ages belong to Him.

The familiar Apostles' Creed used to have it so: "Born of the Virgin Mary, suffered under Pontius Pilate, died and was buried. He descended into Hell and on the third day rose again." The current text reads not "descended into Hell" but "descended to the dead." Language changes. Truth does not. The "harrowing of Hell" refers to Christ's passing this night through the realms of the dead, as the new Catechism has it, "not to descend into Hell to deliver the damned, not to destroy the Hell of damnation, but to free the just who had gone before Him." This fills the mind with questions. Where were the dead all the while? Did they note the passing of time as we do? Does the harrowing of Hell continue in our day as He ransoms those who never knew Him in this life, the good departed? "Harrowing of Hell" is old English for this mystery, harrowing in the sense of despoiling, plundering, robbing Satan of the captive.

Relish the immortal dimension of your life. This is knowledge in grace, the wisdom of the heart. Here is scope to existence, neither fanciful nor imaginative. In the mysteries we celebrate these days, we reach sublimest heights and most terrifying depths. O Holy God, O Holy Mighty God. O Holy Immortal God have mercy on us. Amen.

Faith on the Edge

JOHN 16:12–15

I bind unto myself today
The strong name of the Trinity,
By invocation of the same,
The Three in One, the One in Three.

Of whom all nature hath creation,
Eternal Father, Spirit, Word.
Praise to the Lord of my salvation.
Salvation is of Christ the Lord.

I bind unto myself today
The strong name of the Trinity.
　　　　　—The Breastplate of St. Patrick

A woman named Polly Toynbee, writing for *The Manchester Guardian*, an English newspaper, is much taken by hearing that the Pope is writing an encyclical on superstition. *The Pontifical Commission for Culture* has prepared a report about the dangers of "people believing in magic, levitation, visitation by spirits, aliens, angels and the like."

She then makes it clear how grim the situation is by suggesting the Pope start with "the Turin Shroud, transubstantiation, Virgin visions, stigmata, to say nothing of Ascension and Assumption." Superstition for her covers a lot of territory. The Pope is concerned, she says, "over New Age practices and beliefs in the Church's own convents and monasteries: crystals, pyramids, astrology, psychics, aliens and Eastern mysticism invade the Church. Catholic retreat houses offer aroma therapy, sufi dancing, enneagrams, rebirth techniques and mind expanding techniques."

If Polly is right, there may be need of a letter. Only one in five in Britain believe in God. She says of herself that doctrinal issues are puzzling to an outsider. Outsider or not, she does not hesitate to pronounce freely on that of which she knows nothing. This, of course, makes good copy and papers thrive on such good copy. She is "bemused" by the Eucharist, considers the Pope barbaric in his teaching on contraception and abortion, notes the damage he does. Just when her world was becoming reasonable, it is overwhelmed by the supernatural. She would supplant any credence in the supernatural with truth and empirical evidence.

She has a point, of course, but she doesn't get it. Humankind will believe in something, in anything. We are immortal, whether we agree or not. We will cope with that reality, one way or another, or die in the attempt.

What proves the reality of the Faith as much as the power of its substitutes when true faith is lacking? People will believe in almost anything. Once they have assented to some sort of supernatural dimension in their lives, they will get on with the business of living and do pretty well. The doing pretty well does not prove the verity of their beliefs—it proves that having a belief is natural and healthy.

We as Christians are a bold lot in attesting to what we believe, and as Catholics we are at the head of that lot in the extravagance of our claims. We make more demands on the depth of our faith than any who profess Christ. We never dodge or soften or sidestep the challenge that faith makes on us. The more Catholic you are, the wilder the claims, and the less so, the more remote from the whole truth.

What we expect the faithful to believe is breathtaking. In a word, it is incredible, except in terms of faith, God's grace, the human intellect and will. Our faith is rooted in history, fully consonant with the human intelligence, totally satisfying to the aspirations of the human heart. Our claims are outrageous and we stand by them, always have, continue to do so. And, of course, people like Polly Toynbee are aghast and outraged and continue blind by choice.

So, if you would live dangerously and at the edge, be at home in your faith. Glory in the extravagance of what is asked of us, joyous in your response in the grace of God.

Today, on Trinity Sunday, we are at it again in professing our faith in a God at once Three and One—the Holy Trinity, Father, Son, Holy

Spirit. Here theologians run riot in analyzing what is so totally beyond our comprehension. They talk bravely of one nature, two processions, three persons, four relations, as well as circumincession, co-inherence, hypostatic union, and feel in so doing that they have a hold on mystery.

It is all gift, of course. The human response is essential, but the first move came from God. What follows from the gift is love, love of God and for all. So our faith obliges us by its nature to respond to God for ourselves and for all.

We are beholden for the gift to God Almighty and wholly given to using it for the good of all. To whom much is given, much will be asked. If you do not pray for the world, you are no Christian and certainly no Catholic, for prayer is love manifest.

"The Breastplate of St. Patrick" is also know as "The Deer's Cry"— for Patrick and his band of monks were mistaken for deer when overwhelmed by an ambush of enemies.

> I arise today
> Through a mighty strength,
> The invocation of the Trinity.
> Through belief in the Threeness
> Through confession of the Oneness
> Of the Creator of creation.
>
> I arise today
> Through the strength of heaven
> Light of sun
> Radiance of moon
> Splendor of fire
> Speed of lightning
> Swiftness of wind
> Depth of sea
> Stability of earth
> Firmness of rock.

Mysteries

 ## MARK 4:26–33

One of the problems that people who make encyclopedias face is the enormous growth of human knowledge. It is becoming increasingly difficult to make an attempt at any all-over survey of what is known. Yet, with the growth of knowledge has come also an ability to accumulate it, store it, and retrieve it, and that in an unbelievably small space and in an unbelievably short time. Encyclopedias need no longer be books. They can be stored in a variety of electronic media.

For all that, our competence remains impressively limited and our knowledge thin. Things like time, space, life, the soul, immortality, are not clear to us. Science is great. Greater is philosophy. Greater still is theology. But beyond them all is wisdom, and the wise are few. Wisdom is hard to come by. The reason is that wisdom deals with mystery, and life is full of mystery of which the scientific age is grossly ignorant.

See your dictionary:

"*Time* is a non-spatial continuum in which events occur in apparently irreversible succession from the past through the present to the future." Yet, the question remains: What is time?

"*Space* is the intuition of a three-dimensional field of everyday experience." But what is space?

"*Life* is the property or the quality manifested in functions by which living organisms are distinguished from dead organisms and from inanimate matter." That says very little more than if you not dead you are probably alive.

"*Eternity* is the totality of time without beginning or end." We don't need a dictionary to tell us that.

The words, the notions, the ideas, they are clear enough. We know what they mean. But who can understand any of them? They remain what Catholics call mysteries: truths which are beyond our comprehension. Life is full of them. We forget that because of our familiarity with them. Without knowing much about them, we can make use of them. We know nothing about the ultimate nature of electricity, but that poses no problem. You can turn a light on or off.

It is children who reveal the quest for wisdom in asking exasperating questions that nobody can answer. "Why is light, light? Where is my soul? Why is a dog not something else?" "Go ask your father!"

It seems to be the point of the parables of Jesus. There are so many mysteries that surround you in daily life, and yet you balk when I speak to you of heavenly mysteries. You know nothing at all about what life is in the seed that sprouts, that grows, that matures, that bears fruit. Yet, when I talk of eternal life, the life to come, the Kingdom of God and entering it, your minds cloud over with doubt. The parables are wasted on you. Your ears do not hear. Your eyes do not see. Your hearts do not believe because you do not make the leap of faith.

It is as true today as it was in Christ's day. People don't change much from one generation to the next. The human heart is still hard. We are still deaf, still blind. Were it not so, the world, the whole world, would long since have gone after Christ and become His. It hasn't done so.

And yet the Kingdom is here, it has begun, its life pulses in the human scene in the same mysterious way the life of the seed shares, the tiny mustard seed which contains within it the great shrub it will become. Something within that small kernel of corn emerges as a growing plant, growing every day larger by way of the soil nurtured by sun and rain.

Our skeptical hearts question. We need more evidence. We are not impressed. It is, they tell us, Christianity itself which is making Christ unacceptable, and Christ himself was not accepted. He came on His own terms, not theirs, not His people's. He was not quite what they were looking for. So today. The Church is not quite what they are looking for. Those looking cannot see. They cannot hear. Can anything good come from Nazareth, from Poland?

So we know so little about the simplest things, and we skirt God because He speaks of mysteries, preaches an unworkable gospel, makes unconscionable demands, advances a program too poetic and romantic to be taken seriously.

But not by all. A few listen. A few look. A few take heart because they ponder in silent wonder. They are blessed indeed. The Kingdom is theirs. And, of course, it will not stop there. Seeds grow.

Believing in Love

 MATTHEW 8:28–34
MARK 5:1–20
LUKE 8:26–34

The story of Christ healing the possessed man on the other side of the lake has always had a unique appeal for me, and possibly also for you. In any case, the implications in the tale are many; applications, too, if you like.

To begin with, everything is not clear. In Matthew, the place across the lake is called Gadara, in Mark, Gerasa, in some Luke texts, Gergesa. Nor has the place been accurately sited, as far as I know, for the most likely places have no steep cliff, as the story mentions. Further, in Matthew there are two men, in Mark and Luke, one, though it is obvious that all three gospels deal with the same event. Still, these details do not lessen the impact of the story nor call into question its authenticity.

Christ crosses the little sea and comes ashore. A madman well known in the area starts to scream and shout at Him, asking Him if he had come to make trouble and calling Him the Son of God. This man, or the two of them, wandered among the graves, tormenting themselves and breaking whatever chains people had managed to force upon them lest they do damage to themselves or others. It is a wild scene indeed and we have before us some seriously disturbed people.

That Jesus should come to this particular spot and to this particular tormented man interests us. He asks the unclean spirit to tell his name, and it turns out that there is not one spirit in him but many, a legion of them. Aware that Christ would expel them, they ask that they be sent into a large herd of pigs nearby, two thousand of them, no small number. One wonders why. What advantage was there in entering the pigs, unless perhaps they thought of abiding in them for a long time.

Christ listens to the suggestion of the spirit, an instance of dialogue between good and evil in which Christ responds positively to a suggestion offered. He commands the spirits to come out of the man, they do, and immediately enter the pigs. The pigs forthwith go racing down the hill, truly possessed, and go plunging over the cliff to their deaths in the water below.

Meanwhile, the man has come to himself, is in his right mind, composed, and at peace. We may assume he was naked, so we can see the disciples sharing their clothing with him that he might appear decent.

Talk has gone to the villages and towns nearby and brought a hasty entry on the scene of local people, and, assuredly, the owners of the pigs. They are overwhelmed. For one thing, there is the loss of the herd, certainly worth a vast sum of money. For another, there is the sight of the demented man totally in possession of his faculties.

A normal reaction to goodness is fear, and fear is also a normal reaction to power. When profound goodness is at once manifest, the fear can reach extravagant proportions. It is important to know this. We fear God because He is good, because He is love, and fear Him all over again because He is almighty. If one cannot bear witness to this in oneself, one certainly knows people who are frightened by God, who shy away from grace, who do not want to go near holy people or holy places. Such are literally overcome with fear and cannot cope with it. They may even express their fear in anger and fury.

So they ask Christ to go away, to clear out of the place. There is no discussion about possible settlement for the pigs, no call for explanation and instruction, no invitation to come and heal others in the area. Just go away! Get out of here! Leave us!

On the other hand, there is the healed man. He begs Christ to permit him to join the company and follow Him. The Lord will not have it. "No, You are to go through the ten towns of the area and tell what God has done for you."

Christ leaves. The story is complete. It has been a very baffling event. If we assume that in contemporary terms the pigs were worth, say, fifty dollars each, then we are dealing with a matter of a $100,000 loss. If half that, surely too modest, then $50,000. No trifle. It would seem Christ could be held directly responsible for this loss. This show of power so frightened the people that they could not accept Him.

The unqualified good of the healed man asking to join Christ's company is oddly reversed when he is refused and told to go and wander through the district telling his story of God's goodness to him.

Were these people Jews? What business had they raising pigs? Did Christ punish them by destroying their herd? This is surely contradictory to His manner of acting. He was not one to punish, to afflict, to harm, even when such action was justified.

We could spend hours wondering about this whole episode and really not come up with anything worthwhile. It seems an unusual manifestation of the power of God in Jesus Christ, in a most frightening way, and it reveals human reaction to such a display.

Hostility, fear, rejection, indifference, seem to me normal responses to the presence of God. It is good to reflect on this and to be able to understand what happens.

When we speak of God, when we reveal Him, it must not be thought at once that hostility, fear, rejection, or indifference indicate that we have not communicated well or that the reaction has been unacceptable. We may have communicated very well, the hearers may know exactly what we mean, and they may not be able to cope with it. So, they become hostile or frightened. They reject what we offer or fall asleep or something similar.

In dealing with the human heart, God may find the same scenario. If you look into your own heart's life, I daresay you have, as I have, answered God now in one way, now in another, but in some cases negatively. This is not because we have failed to understand Him, or that we did not want to respond, but by being overwhelmed we were simply not capable of anything else.

In which case, what does God do? He waits and comes back later. He is not easily discouraged. He will keep this up for a lifetime if need be. He never gives up. Hostility, fear, rejection, and indifference are not rare at all in our relationship to God. They are common. The disciples did not fall asleep at Gethsemani or at Tabor because they were tired. No. They were simply overcome, overwhelmed, and could not cope. So they turned off and went to sleep.

There was a monk at this abbey who consistently fell asleep at the abbot's chapter talks. That is one way of handling an abbot. He even snored till is neighbors nudged him.

The point is, I think, not to deny hostility, fear, rejection, and indifference, bur rather to recognize what is going on. Hostility need not indicate disagreement or conflict at all. Nor need fear mean that one cannot trust, but only that one cannot do so at the moment. Rejection is not rejection. It is just a way of getting rid of someone at the door you are not willing, able, or ready to admit. Indifference is perhaps a more subtle approach, but indicates anything but indifference.

All of this explains why we are at such pains to make God predictable, manageable, someone with whom we can deal. An unpredictable, unmanageable God is far more than we can live with. We like structure, routine, rubric, regularity, and order in our lives. We expect God to arrive that way. Let Him come in sacrament and worship, let Him arrive on time, in proper context, in good order.

But let there be chaos, disruption, upheaval, the unusual, the untoward, and the unexpected, and we are quite unnerved. We panic, and in panic we call on anything that will sustain us: hostility, fear, rejection, and indifference.

Our own times are characterized by a considerable degree of chaos in many areas, and I refer particularly to western society. When I was in Papua New Guinea, it was easy to trace the local response to the coming, the settling, the dominance of the European in those islands: hostility, fear, rejection, indifference.

I left Papua New Guinea in 1951, having arrived the first time in 1948. I returned twenty-five years later at Christmas, 1973. The first reaction after so long an interval was really a shocking experience in many ways. The changes were simply staggering. Yet of all those impression, one was outstanding.

The face of the people had changed. The face had softened. The face of the Papua New Guinean man and woman was no longer strained, tightened, taut, frightened, worried. Rather, calm, peace, and joy had entered their spirit and come out on their faces. It was unmistakable. I had known them before. I see them now. There is no similarity.

I concluded that they have come to realize that in back of everything is love, and the love is the love of God. To be sure, health, education, work, income, competence, confidence—all these have their share. But the fundament, believe me, is the faith which assures them of the love of God.

When God is hard on you, when He is unpredictable, unreliable, unfathomable, unreasonable, outrageous, and what all else, one can understand if you are hostile, or fearful or rejecting or feigning indifference. Maybe that is the best you can do at the time. But the healing comes in an ever deepening awareness of His love for each human. This is the only answer. It has a significance beyond all telling.

Christ went sailing across the sea of Galilee, the humble, gentle, loving Jesus. He stepped ashore into a chaotic scene where a madman, perhaps two of them, raved as a maniac among tombs and desolate places, shrieking and howling, acting in a totally mad manner. Christ drove what was tormenting this human out of him, and in doing so released Satanic fury into a vast herd of swine which at once took off down a hill in a frenzied race over the edge of a cliff to their deaths in the sea below. One mad scene replaced by one more mad.

Here is a confrontation divine and diabolic, divine and human, on a splendid scale. It does not surprise us that hostility follows, as well as rejection, fear, and indifference. No wonder they tell Jesus, "Get out of here, leave us!"

Jesus is not hurt. He leaves as quietly as he came, but leaves behind one healed and whole. He told him to walk through the towns to the end of his days to tell the message to all: God is good and God loves.

There may come a day when chaos becomes the characteristic of your own inner landscape. Your reactions are predictable. Let them be. The recovery comes in the growing awareness that despite all the evidence to the contrary, God is good and does love us, that we are called upon to believe in it. Believing in love is without question the greatest, most noble, most significant work a human can do. In the grace of God we can do that work. It is worth doing.

3 ~ Jesus

The Hidden Christ

JOHN 1:29–34

> The next day he saw Jesus coming toward him and
>   declared, "Here
> is the Lamb of God who takes away the sin of the
>   world. I myself did
> not know him, but the one who sent me to baptize
>   with water said to me,
> 'He on whom you see the Spirit descend and remain
>   is the one who baptizes
> with the Holy Spirit.' And I myself have seen and
>   have testified that this
> is the Son of God." (John 1)

Jesus was the hidden God. John did not know Him. They did not grow up together. John had spent his life in the desert; now like Jesus, about thirty years old. All his days in the desert prepared him and those he preached to, for this signal event, so long waited for, yet inevitably to come to pass, in secret, all hidden until the time came.

Christmas is known and celebrated all over the world. Yet, in all this celebration Jesus may indeed be a hidden God. In all of the Christmas trees, Christmas decorations, Christmas cards, Christmas shopping, Christmas greens, and Christmas parties, one may be hard pressed to find Jesus. It is permitted in the state, the county, the town, to do everything for Christmas, but no crib, no creche, no manger, no Mother and Child, no Joseph and shepherds and wise men, on public property. They must be hidden.

It can be a bit puzzling. Advent is smothered in a Christmas season that long predates Christmas. St. Nicholas gets mixed up in it all by way of a fairy tale Santa that has nothing to do with the original save the name, and he had nothing to do with Christmas. The gifts of the Magi on Epiphany are moved ahead to Christmas day. So the whole is confused and distorted. It can be exasperating. Some are sorely tempted to dismiss the whole as commercialism triumphant world wide.

Maybe.

Perhaps if we heed the Spirit like John, the hidden Jesus may be manifest beneath it all, in it all. This is a season for family gathering, for children, for reconciliation with God and one another, for mercy and compassion on the needy. There is more kindness and mercy. There is something in the air. There is something going on beneath, behind, hidden in it all. The Spirit can reveal Jesus in it if we listen, if we are open and aware. We can penetrate glitter and tinsel and reach the Crib, in the human heart, in the human scene.

The Christian mystery is always going to involve a difficult response to the Spirit, and that in every scene and situation. Christ remains a hidden God, but not an absent one.

He was hidden in the cave at Bethlehem in the midst of a world that did not know His presence, yet the Spirit revealed Him even to the poor and inconsequential, to the inadequate wisdom of the East in the Magi. When the time came, John made Him known even though he did not know Him. The Spirit revealed to John.

The Spirit reveals to us and to all if we listen. It was just as hard to recognize Jesus in Israel as it is for us in Bardstown or in our own hearts. He is in our times, is present in our days, revealed by the Spirit in His Church, in His disciples, in His word and sacrament. The world did not go running after Jesus when He came, although He was manifest by the Spirit. It is no different today. The world does not flock to His Church. Yet, the Spirit reveals Him as there, truly there.

That being so, we ought not be surprised that Christ is so hard to find in Christmas. He has always been hard to find, not such much because He is hidden, but because we do not see in the light of the Spirit.

How great our joy then in the Spirit to know that He has come, that He lives among us and loves us. He is revealed ever so subtly, so gently, in the good that people do, in kindness and mercy, in forgiveness and generosity, in concern for the poor, the sick, the afflicted and addicted. It is all the work of the Spirit manifesting Jesus. How poignant, pitiful, His presence in all who suffer. They are a multitude.

Deus absconditus: O hidden God, be manifest to us and to all. Surely, too, we can pray that our celebration of the Christian mysteries may become more worthy, endowed with more grace and beauty, be more intelligent and perceptive, that the hidden Christ may be fully revealed in the Spirit.

Trees

LUKE 1:26–38

Yesterday, maybe, or tomorrow, some monks will go out and look for a Christmas tree, a green tree, an evergreen, green for life, for hope, but a tree. On it they will hang red apples or a reasonable facsimile. The coming of Christ is threefold. He came in history nineteen thousand years ago. He comes to each of us personally. He will come at the end of time. The tree has a threefold significance, too. It is the first tree in the Garden of Eden, the tree on which hung the beautiful but forbidden fruit, traditionally an apple. It is tree we use to celebrate the coming of Christ. Finally, it is the tree on which Christ died, on which he will hang as fruit, red with His blood.

On this Christmas tree, beside the red fruit, we string lights, for Christ is the light come into our darkness. He is the light of the world, the dawn in the east, the rising sun, the splendor of the Father. Christ was born at the winter solstice, the darkest day of the year when the sun is lowest in our skies, the day when the sun ceases in its descent, pauses, and begins a return. The days now grow longer. It is the dawn of light, and Christ is that dawn.

One ought never to explain symbols. It a sense, that spoils them. One should never explain a fairy tale to a child. If the child does not get the point, wait a while. In a year he or she will get it at once. The child has to be ready for it; the response must come from within. It is only when people are so removed from reality, so impoverished as to be out of touch with their own depths, that we are reduced to manuals explaining every aspect of liturgy. All is interpreted, laid out in the open. It is itself a commentary on a time too rational, too practical, too sensible, whose depth is mere emotion and feeling, sentimental, undeveloped response. New Age spirituality, however inappropriate, is an over-reaction to a too intellectual religiosity. Yet, it is sometimes necessary to prime the pump and encourage a faith in ourselves and our resources. At least we can cultivate the love of quiet and of pondering.

People in Ireland some three thousand years before Christ built massive mounds of stone, hills with a hidden, inner chamber for the dead. The blind entry passage had a slot over the barred door that admitted sunlight, sunlight which at Newgrange on December 21, the winter solstice, would pass through the slot, go down the corridor and flood the inmost chamber with light, once a year.

What an observant people! How carefully they watched the movement of sun and moon and stars. How shrewd in their ability to build a small hill and equip it with so elaborate a design. Much of the interior was carved with intricate patterns.

What were they saying in all of this if not expressing hunger for light, not merely the phases of the sun's light, the moon's light, the light of the stars, but a different light that would never be overcome with darkness. Surely this is all prophetic, this is the human heart dreaming of a Coming Day which would know no end, the perpetual light to which we commend our dead.

It is to be noted, of course, that all this is for northern latitudes, whose winter knows no green, enters into long nights and short days this season. It does not follow that lower latitudes and people on the other side of the world have no way of saying what we say. Christ is for all, for everyone, everywhere. Every people, every culture, can speak its own language, use its own symbols, to express realities beyond words. So humans speak, so we relate, communicate. Poinsettias grow wild in the tropics, an appropriate Christmas flower. We need be constant against perverse trends in the human to trivialize the sacred, to make the holy banal, common. We like to destroy the sacrament of our lives. There is no aspect of our existence that we do not cheapen or vulgarize. Shallow living means no respect for depth. But to travel in shallow waters is fatal. Sooner or later you run aground. Happiness lies in deep waters. In staying in touch with our deeps we truly live. It is through the material that we express the spiritual. We know no other way.

All is holy. Because bread is holy, we have the Divine Bread. Because wine is holy, the Cup is sacred. Because this house is holy, every house is. The green tree, the rising sun, light out of darkness, birth and death are holy, touched with the Divine. His coming makes this so. And He is near, very near.

Living by Our True Nature

MATTHEW 3:1–12

The second Sunday in Advent opens with a messianic poem from Isaias describing the figure who is to come from David's line. He will be filled with the spirit of the prophets. He will establish a new society reflecting God's sanctity on earth. He will restore the peace of Eden. The same Spirit that hovered over all at the beginning, the Spirit that gave all creatures life, inspired the Judges and Saul, gives craftsmen their skill, gives leaders discretion, inspires the prophets. The same Spirit rests on the Messiah and in His era will be poured out on all. So the Messiah has the wisdom of Solomon, the heroism of David, the knowledge and fear of God in patriarch and prophet, in Moses, Jacob, and Abraham.

The description of the Spirit's gifts described by Isaiah became our gifts of the Holy Spirit, seen now not merely for the Messiah, but for all the people of God; indeed, through them to spread out through all the world.

Our world is filled with the glory of God, the fruit of the Spirit manifest in compassion, in mercy, in healing. How great the glory of God in all who manifest the Spirit in love for the poor, the imprisoned, the addicted, the afflicted, in the cause of peace and justice.

Surely the Spirit is manifest in art and beauty, in communications, in the grandeur of a suspension bridge, an airliner, a mighty ship. The marvels in sight and in sound and how much else are surely the fruit of God's Spirit active in the world.

If we are called on to recognize the Spirit in Christ and see Him as He who is to come, and if we are called in Faith to receive the Spirit and manifest His presence by our own lives in the world—are we not also bidden to have eyes of faith that see God revealed in the glorious works wrought through humankind? The more so if others do not. How great the glory of God in what He has done and in what He continues to do through creation and creatures.

We cannot assume that once the world was brought to be that God left it. How much easier to believe He continues in it and specifically in His Son and those in love with His Son, and through them in all the world. We are Catholic.

But the Gospel reading today is troubling. John the Baptist castigates some who came to him. He called them a brood of vipers, snakes, serpents. What is evil about a viper that one is condemned by such identification? Nothing really. Vipers are not evil, we are. We think of the viper as evil because of its deadly poison, but it is not, not really. The Genesis story identifies the Evil One in the form of a snake, and by way of the snake the Evil One tempted Eve. Because the snake is low, secretive, sudden, and dangerous, it makes a fitting player for Satan. Yet the snake is not evil, Satan is.

So we can understand the rest of Isaiah this morning in his describing an Eden, a Paradise to come in which the wolf will live with the lamb, the panther lie down with the goat. The cow and the bear will graze, the lion will eat hay like an ox, and the infant will play over the den of the adder.

Here is high poetry driving home a hard lesson, for no wolf will live with the lamb. It is not the way of wolves. No panther lie down with the goat. Panthers do not live so. The are wild animals and their lives are violent. The handsome wolf kills the beautiful deer for food. It is his nature. He is not evil. He fulfills the law of his being.

We are evil, which is what Isaiah is saying. We are not violent by nature. We do not live by killing one another. Called to be good, though, we lust and rape, we steal and defraud, we bomb and burn. It is our past-time, our hobby, our business, our method.

The Messiah came to live among us, richly endowed with the Spirit. It did not take Him long to find out what we are like. Yet, He turned tragedy into a triumph of mercy and forgiveness, of resurrection and eternal life. Although the wolf will no doubt live with the lamb before we beat our swords into ploughshares and our spears into sickles, we are none the less called to live our true nature, as humans, as immortal. We need not be a brood of vipers. The Spirit hovers over us, is active in us. If we acknowledge His presence and His power, respond to Him in our lives and in our world, then we participate in the Kingdom Christ came to build.

Christmas Morning

Our first overseas visitor after World War II to the seminary I attended was a distinguished doctor of theology. He was full of self-assurance and confidence, did not hesitate to make his views known. Some of the Fathers picked him up at Notre Dame to bring him to the major seminary near Chicago. On the way they asked him what he thought of Notre Dame. "A kindergarten," he said. A bit of a savage remark, to be sure. But what he was saying was, "What was Notre Dame to some European university going back to the Middle Ages, a place of magnificent stone chapels and halls of splendid beauty. Through them had gone popes, cardinals, bishops, doctors in theology in numbers, as well as canonized saints." He was talking about the whole tremendous impact of history. Next to that, Notre Dame wasn't much. Granted, but still it is a great university, as good as any in Europe. Lacking in history yes, but if you insist on that you miss the whole.

So he came to Techny, our place. They showed him the chapel, something of which they were proud: steel frame, brick facing, ceilings, arches, a contemporary structure, for all its beauty. He took one look and dismissed it with a shrug: kitsch, a German word for something tacky, cheesy, impermanent, stage scenery. Granted. But, the chapel was a vibrant center for a vigorous religious community, filled many times a day for common prayer, a setting for vows, for priestly ordinations, and bishops' consecrations, as well as mission departures to every part of the world. If you missed that, you missed the whole. Architecture was a modest aspect.

We have to be careful with Christmas. We may be like the German theologian, so learned and competent, and survey the whole Christmas scene and dismiss it as too commercial, too tawdry, what with buying and selling, the whole matter of gifts given and received, decorations of light and trees and Santas, the music of carols, the excitement in the air, Christmas bonuses and vacations, gatherings for dinners for parties. By the time Christmas comes we are nearly exhausted and glad when it is over.

That being so, one is tempted to see the whole in something of a Scrooge mood. It's all humbug, just business, money, and commerce.

Maybe, if you want it to be that way. But there is no need. One can go deeper, crack the shell, find the meat, and know the real joy of it all.

It is, after all, the most important moment in human history, the birth of Jesus Christ, son of Mary, son of God, in a shelter for animals, a cave in the hills outside Bethlehem. This is the heart of it all, the point. He came for us, for love of us, for the salvation of the world. He makes known to us in clear terms our destiny as immortals, the Kingdom of Heaven, now open to all.

He is not just another Buddha or Confucius or Mohammed, great men all in the providence of God. He was not just a great teacher, a splendid healer, a moral leader. He is all of those and more. He is unique. There is no other name under Heaven by which we are saved. He is God from God, Light from Light, True God from True God, born of a virgin, who came for our salvation. For us He was crucified, suffered, died and was buried. On the third day he rose again to lead us all to the Father and eternal glory. He left us His Church, His presence on earth, to carry on what He was, what He said, what He did, and in grace unites us with Him to love Him now and forever. By his death he draws from all the evil in us, forgives our sins that put Him to death, and embraces us in love in His sacramental presence.

Ponder these things. Dwell on these mysterious truths. To do so is good for you. There is nothing better, for in doing so you live in touch with the whole of your being, mortal and immortal, of earth and for heaven. When we take seriously these realities we touch the source of true happiness and peace. They give life meaning and purpose, joy and substance. To live without such faith makes life dismal and pointless, in many ways absurd and shallow.

In other words, make the most of Christmas, draw deeply from the well of divine mystery, and drink the water of life.

There was a tree in the Garden of Eden bearing fruit they were told not to eat yet. The primal disobedience turned the tree into a tree of death. Now there is a new green tree, the red fruit of His blood staining it for us, and it becomes the tree of life for all the world until the end of time.

The birth was humble and hidden, but the angels knew and sang glorious music for the poor shepherds. They told them to go see, and they did. A beautiful star shone in the sky and the high and mighty, knowing what it meant by grace, came from afar to do homage and offer royal gifts. King Herod heard of the new born king and offered a different response, tried to kill him.

We join the angels, the shepherds, the three kings, and offer our love to the Holy Child. We come to mass, Christmas Mass, and thank him for coming. God bless you all, for blessed you are, blessed many times over.

Christmas Mass at Dawn

The December issue of *Popular Mechanics* featured an article on the Seven Wonders of the Modern World. The American Society of Engineers took part in a survey to list what the members thought were the greatest achievements in the world of human enterprise. The list included seven: the Panama Canal, the Empire State Building in New York, the Golden Gate Bridge in San Francisco, the Canadian National Tower in Toronto, the tunnel beneath the English Channel, the Dutch wall against the North Sea, the five mile dam on the Parana River in Brazil/Paraguay. Some of them are well known to us, some not. All are magnificent. What is notable is that of the seven, four are concerned with communication: the Panama Canal, the Golden Gate Bridge, the Canadian tower, the Channel tunnel. Communication is important to us: to cross from the Atlantic to the Pacific, to cross the bay in San Francisco, to cross the channel from England to France, to send radio signals across the continent and a world. The complex network of communication among us is unbelievably large. The air is constantly full of messages.

The Son of God is called the Word of God. He is the communication of the Father. The Father sent his Word to us. The angels sang in the night, "We bring you tidings of great joy." The angels themselves are messengers, bring us gospel, which means good news. To evangelize is to spread the gospel and so pass on this good word. It is clear that in the world of faith, we communicate. We are not only in touch with one another—see send greetings at Christmas—but we commune with God and He with us. Messages to God are rites and symbolic actions, love expressed in sign and gesture. We communicate with God in prayer, and He with us in Christ, the Word of God.

Christmas is the beginning of this new kind of communication with God. We read God in Christ and hear Him. What we read is good news and what we hear is worth listening to, our salvation.

It all has meaning. It makes sense, ultimately. Life matters because love matters and love matters because it is the key. We know something of human love and human love can be very beautiful. We know something of divine love in Jesus Christ born on Christmas Day. It is a superbly beautiful love.

What then will ultimate glory be? What is the revelation to come when this womb opens and we pass through to eternal life?

Christmas green is for life and hope, and Christmas red is for the heart of love, the fruit of the tree. Christmas is a communication feast. It is an exchange of gifts. He gives Himself to us—the good Word of God—and we give ourselves to Him, the human answer, the returned greeting, the responsive word.

What humans have achieved in crossing great bodies of water, in linking oceans and continents, in sending speech across the world is great. Who would deny it? All to the glory of God made manifest in the works of man, a communication of God.

Yet what is all this to bridging the chasm between God and humankind, between time and eternity, Heaven and earth? Here is achievement indeed. Jesus is a person, human and divine. "For mercy has a human heart, pity a human face, and love the human born divine."

No wonder Christ is called bridge builder, pontifex, pontiff, and the same title held in honor by the successor of Peter, Christ's vicar, in the chair in Rome. Bridge builder indeed. Supreme pontiff, in the person of Christ, divine Lord.

May the traffic on that bridge be heavy, for it is not mere beauty to behold, but beauty to embrace in love. So give glory to God in Heaven who gave glory to God on earth in His coming. O wonderful exchange. O wonder of our modern world, Christ, the Word made flesh, the child, born of Mary.

The New Gospel

LUKE 1:1–4; 4:14–21

People not much different from ourselves lived in generations past quite comfortably with slavery. We find that odd. People not much different from ourselves lived in generations past quite comfortably with injustice to blacks. We find that odd, too. I suppose generations to come will find it odd that we could rest so comfortably in a nuclear age with doom and disaster at our fingertips. Certainly we will be thought odd who are so at ease with a divided faith, with a dismembered body, to all appearances, so grossly contrary to Christ's wish and will. We do not lie awake at night grieving over it. Surely the nursery rhyme is about the Church, the cosmic egg, the future of the world, the perfect and incredible egg. Once its integrity was broken, all the king's horses and all the king's men could not put it together again.

Pastors did not scold their people or their society in the days of slavery. It would have been thought inappropriate. Priests did not scold their people nor upbraid them and their society for their treatment of blacks. Indeed, they may have had slaves or have segregated blacks. No one today seems unduly shocked and scandalized at the mockery made of Christ's Church by a horde of dissident disciples who agree to disagree. We put men and women to death for betraying their country. We would not think in such terms for schism. Granted that there has been an ugly strain of anti-Semitism among certain peoples at certain times, was there any continued outcry against this sin from the pulpit? One does not sense that.

It is in the light of such notions that we must see Christ today and listen to Him as He responds to a request for some word and comment in the synagogue gathering. He takes the scroll, unrolls it, finds His

84

place, reads the passage, rolls up the manuscript, gives it to the attendant and sits down. All eyes are on Him. It is a great moment.

When Christ talks, preaches, and instructs, He is at once compelling, fearless, and outrageous. He is spell-binding for His grasp of truth, ardent in His expression of it, and heedless of what may follow. "No man has ever spoken as this man." Everywhere He went, he made friends and enemies.

He came not only with a new Gospel, but with a new dispensation, a new covenant. He declared the end of the Old Law, the birth of the New. Now Israel and the Kingdom of God were no longer between the Mediterranean Sea and the Jordan River. Israel was now the whole world. "The Kingdom of God has come, and you are witnesses to it."

Nothing like this had ever been heard before. It was both devastating and delightful. It aroused enthusiastic response and lethal hatred. It was fire on the earth that enlightened, burned, warmed, and consumed.

The whole Gospel message is of a kind, but we are used to it. The words are familiar to us. Our preaching is gentle. We do not choose to upset, to enrage. People rarely walk out in fury at what we say, at what we teach.

Still, take care. The Gospel is dynamite still. It is power. The sacraments are divine. A little bread, a little wine, is room enough for divinity. Christ did more than talk, and if His talk ennobled and inspired, His deeds brought divine life into human life. Our Christian life is not merely hearing and reading words, but doing the Christ thing: putting Him to death, witnessing His rising, receiving His Spirit. All of that brings into the human scene a divine element that is at work, despite human frailty and stupidity. Like some hidden power in the earth, in the sea, in the air, that once and again suddenly reveals itself in strength. So Christ simmers below the surface of all that is.

To be in touch with that Christ means to participate in the new creation of the new world, to build the Kingdom of God with Him, not on our designs, but His, not according to our dreams and plans. It is far more than that, far more in every way. "Eye has not seen, ear has not heard, nor has it so much as entered the heart of man what God prepares."

That is what He began when He unrolled the scroll. How they loved it. How they hated it. How much love do you have? How much hate? If you are human, probably significant amounts of both. Look in your heart and see.

So, response to Christ in our day is not much different from the response He met long ago. People leave and do not come back anymore. They go elsewhere, if they go anywhere. If this be on the quiet side, a brief dip into history reveals outrageous hatred of the Church expressed in violence and destruction, persecution and oppression of all kind.

Although it makes us uncomfortable at times, the Word of God is powerful and it will triumph.

He is Come

ISAIAH 66:10–14
GALATIANS 6:14–18
LUKE 10:1–12, 17–20

We might see these readings as a set of three panels, a triptych, the large one in the center, the two others to each side.

In the center, Christ is sending out disciples two by two. To the left is Isaiah and the Mother love of Jerusalem. To the right, we see St. Paul and his stress on Christ's passion and death, the glory of the cross.

Those who are disenchanted with what they call "organized religion" run into trouble rather early, for Christianity is organized. Out of the earliest disciples He chose twelve. Out of the twelve apostles He chose one as leader. In the reading today He sends out seventy-two disciples. The number is of interest. First of all, it was so large that those closest to Him must have been impressed that He stressed the need of prayer, the dearth of workers, and the needs of the harvest. Seventy-two is few in face of the conversion of Israel and the world, a rather modest number. But there is more to it than that. Seventy-two is six dozen, and so we are on touch with the ancient love of numbers and their significance. Three is a spiritual number, and here we have multiples of three. Seven and two adds up to nine. Though this may be a nicety that was added, the point is more than nice, for we are engaged in a *spiritual* endeavor, and there is a basic plan. They are to go ahead to places where He intends to go later. Prepared the ground. Set the scene. Their engagement is a special one. No socializing, visiting, stopping along the way to exchange pleasantries, no passing from house to house in friendly encounter. Take no staff; you are not leading sheep or cattle. You have work to do. No sandals, for they are reserved by the poor for special occasions. Take no provisions, for you are prophets and a prophet is worthy of his hire. What are you to do? Give the word. And what is the word? "He is come!"

Months before D-Day, the Germans and their forces were lined all along the Normandy coast, trying to figure out where the landing would be, for they knew it was coming. They never did find out. They claimed they did, but they only guessed, and they guessed wrong. One who lived through it all, recalled much later his first reaction. He was on top of the cliff very early in the morning with his binoculars, watching the sea. As he watched, he suddenly saw on the horizon tiny black dots, dozens and dozens of them, then hundreds. He turned to his mate and said to him and to himself, "Sie kommen, Sie kommen." They are coming. What a moment! How laden with history. It was one of the greatest military exploits of all time.

So Israel is also filled with expectancy. The air was light with it. Watching, waiting for the One to come. Now men come, two by two with a word, "He has come!" The response would have been electric. Who is he? Where is he from? What is he like? What does he say? What does he do? The seventy-two prepare the way. Soon you will see Him, for He is coming. Hear Him. This is an engagement with the greatest event in history.

The other readings for today describe it: the love of God, the love of the Holy City, Jerusalem, the love of Israel, the Church. The love of God is a love that is beyond us and begs comparison. It is like mother-love. Israelis weaned late. So many of them would remember the warm breast and the suckling at milk. In any case, family life, village life, would commonly have had mothers with babies at their breast. They would be embracing them and fondling them dearly. Such scenes would call up memories, conscious or unconscious, of motherly love, so apt a figure of the love of God, of Israel, of Jerusalem, of the Church, of Christ.

But on the other side, in the other panel, the other reading, we have the dark side, St. Paul and the Cross, and the centrality of the passion and death by which we are redeemed. This is the great stumbling block, the tragic event that earlier followers found so hard to accept. A crucified Messiah? No! That was not their dream. This was the dark side of God's love, or better, the dark side of the human response to God's love. It is an unfathomable mystery: Love came, and we killed Him.

The Good News so ended? Not quite. The end was not passion and death, but rising in glory, and the return to the Father and the sending of the Spirit.

The Cross continues to be a mystery. The role of suffering is an impenetrable darkness. Who can understand it? But, in Christ we can pass through it to glory. God's love is the sweetness of milk at the warm breast. So, too is the Church, yet that mother is the mother of sorrows with a broken heart.

Looking at this, pondering on these things, these events, is beyond our depth indeed, but their very depths respond to our own deeps. For we are deep: our names are written in Heaven.

The apostolic dimension of the Church remains central. In our own day we see a magnificent witness to that in Pope John Paul going to every corner of the world with the word, "He is come!"

The Lord of Glory

 Jesus Christ is the Lord of glory, one with the Father and the Spirit, King of all the Angels and Saints, immortal, everlasting God, Lord of the universe, without beginning or end. He is the new Adam, the firstborn of all creation, embracing in Himself everyone born, past, present, and to come.

His coming was prepared through a long story of a special people chosen for that very purpose, working out in the providence of God a model myth of all our search for God and God's search for us. God came in time, born of a Virgin, lived, taught, did good, suffered, was put to death, rose again after three days, ascended to His Father.

In that redemptive work everyone is involved, for every birth, every death, all suffering and pain, every tear, all laughter, labor, living and loving is now of a new character because the Son of God become the Son of Man has entered into the human scene. Now everything is changed. Everything earthly becomes heavenly, all is opened up, given an eternal dimension. Life has a new meaning, a purpose which enters into it no matter what form or shape it takes.

This is the dream of the ages come true. Myth, legend, poem, song, and rite were trying in this way and that to see this, say this, be this. In response to the Divine light that never wholly disappeared from the human heart despite the first sin, we tried desperately to interpret, to fathom, to understand life, role, and destiny.

We gave expression to that search in countless modes, the fruits of poets and prophets, priests and dreamers, shamans and gurus from time immemorial. Christ and his divine drama are the perfect answer to every one of them. In Him all are fulfilled, made perfect, complete.

Everyone shares in this divine drama, for Christ has entered into everyone. There is no birth that is not a birth of Christ in some fashion, no death that is not a participation in His death. Everything that enters into our life on earth enters this drama of the ages. Yes, even our sins enter it, for our sins are but the gropings, the wanderings, the stumbling in the dark of one seeking happiness and looking for it where it is not.

All suffering is a share in the suffering of Christ, so that not a single tear is lost. All human joy, no matter how light and ephemeral, how passing or futile, is in some way a share in the joy of Christ, the ultimate rapture of God's all-consuming, ravishing love. Few know this, of course. Few are aware. Most are unconscious. Most do not believe. Still, Christ took care through the Church that His word would never disappear from the earth, that His life and death and rising would always live on in rite and reality.

Further, the Word was out, the invitation extended to all at large to enter into union with Him in a living, conscious way, so that life on earth might take on meaning and purpose, share in some sense the original glory that it had in the beginning before the Fall. He never thought many would believe, never said that all would receive him, save at the very end. But the door is always open, the invitation stands. To refuse it deliberately and knowingly is to sin, is to reject light and love. Since the first sin we have preferred darkness to light, evil to good. Christ knows that, for we killed Him because he was good.

Even so, His love is not withdrawn, His message is not restricted. There is no one, not one, of all that have been, that are, and will be, who is not loved by Divine love. That few know of His love is a pity, but not the point. Where there is life, there is love. Those who know of His love accept it, respond to it, enter consciously into the divine drama of redemption and have some grasp of what is going on, enter into the Christ's work. Those who do not, share in the action none the less, even though unconsciously. They live in darkness, ignorance, unaware of the significance of things. But their life is not wasted and useless, for all that entered into it is precious by the life of Christ. By His breath He made every human breath of moment.

One would hope that all will be saved, not by their merits but by Christ's, and by Christ involving all humankind in His redemptive work. The passion and death of the Lord never end on earth, for they live on in sacrament and humanity, even if few know. Precious few knew what was going on the first Good Friday. Precious few know today what is really going on. To know, which is to say, to believe, is to be conscious, to be aware, alive to reality. We are thus redeemed together, one through the other, all through Christ. I share all men's pain and trial and trouble and they, mine, because we all share Christ's. And the joys, too.

The rising and setting of the sun is communal. Grace, like light, is everywhere, not diminished for being shared. It is because human life is holy that it will be received into the kingdom, made holy by Christ. To live without this vision, without this awareness, this consciousness, is to live in Hell, in darkness. With this vision any life is possible; without some share in it, none. To sin is to choose not to live, to hate light, to reject love. Hell does not follow; it is hell already, life without meaning. Christ taught us how to live in a way that would keep alive the vision, pointed out what would lead to the death of light, marked out what would nurture and sustain it.

In the company of believers, He shares His life and death in a profoundly intimate manner, uniting all in close, conscious union with Him and His work for all mankind. These do not form an exclusive elite, for they are no better than anyone else, but their eyes have been opened, they see. They have broken the shell and stepped into reality. Everyone shares some participation in this light, it is in Christ that one enters into a full vision. It follows that those who have the light do all in their power to share it, most of all by their own joy in it.

There is some great significance to the life of faith on earth, for Christ attaches great meaning to it. Though beyond death, there is apparently some manner of making up for what one did not do on earth, it seems clear that the life of faith on earth has a special role in the world's redemption. It does not follow that those who without blame have never been able to enter into the fullness of revelation will therefore be deprived of ultimate happiness. None are outside the kingdom of God's love. It does seem, though, that the Lord in His providence sees to it that there is always present on earth a body of believers who enter deeply and consciously into the Divine drama. That this body of believers should constantly grow and expand is a demand of Christ, yet this demand depends on free response. The Church at times is strong and widespread, at times weak and small. Its presence on earth till the end, however, is a Divine promise.

Just as every human life is touched with suffering in large or small measure, so too the life of the Christian and the life of the Church. In the case of Christian suffering, however, one enters on a profound mystery, where there is a sharing in the suffering of Christ, as well as in the conflict he endured, and in the manner of Christ, rise again. As it was with Christ, so with the Church and often with the follower of Christ: those who oppose and afflict are not aware of what they do. It is this awareness, this consciousness, this grasp of wholeness through faith that constantly emerges as a theme. It is further the same awareness that integrates the aspects of life, pulling together time and eternity, heaven and earth, suffering and joy, action and contemplation, giving and receiving.

Faith, at the same time, embraces past, present, and future, all human efforts to move above and beyond the here and the now, the passing, the earth-bound, society without vision. It is the final resolution that poses most questions: the ultimate triumph of good over evil, the banishment of the spirits of evil, the separation of all who reject love. That there is a Hell, we know. Whether any human is there or not or will be, we do not know. That one can choose Hell, we also know. We know further of some transitory stage where one is willingly obliged to fill up what is lacking by some form of suffering. We are in communion with them through love. We know, too, that here on earth, we are in union with God through Christ, the Father, and the Holy Spirit, but also with the Mother of Christ, the angels, the blessed in Heaven. Thus, this world to the next, elevating our human kinship to its eternal dimension. The union with all humankind, past, present and to come in this way, on a deeper level, embraces all in God.

Paschal Vigil

In his drama, Shakespeare frequently followed serious, tragic scenes with light, humorous ones. By way of contrast, the tragic seemed more tragic, the comic more humorous. So now this night, we put darkness and light together. We come to appreciate more the density of our sinful situation, the glory of the risen light of the redeeming Christ.

Within the span of only three days we have witnessed the most wretched scene history has known when we put the Christ of God to death on the tree. That is followed so soon after by the triumph of saving love in the resurrection, the most significant event in the world.

Sin has done the worst of which it was capable. The divine response was healing in a forgiving love that conquered sin, death, and darkness.

But there is another contrast that is the juxtaposition of time and eternity. Here the two are laid one against the other and so point up the transience of time, the now of eternity.

This is no commemoration service in which we devoutly recall past events. Quite the contrary, we witness to the original event, more than witnesses—we are involved. We share in the death and share in the rising because our sins are involved.

This is no replay of Calvary. We do not run through it again each year at this holy season. There is but one death and rising. The events are transcendent, they ignore time, they are present in God's eternal now. In that now we briefly share when we move onto the stage of these events. We are out of time. We taste eternity. Indeed, we do so in every Eucharist. But, in this holy time, the Paschal Vigil, more profoundly, more dramatically.

The implications are worth a note. We recall the *Apostles' Creed*, the prayer we used more frequently in the past than now. "I believe in God the Father Almighty, maker of Heaven and earth, and in Jesus Christ, His only Son, our Lord, who was conceived of the Holy Spirit, born of the Virgin Mary, suffered, died, was buried, descended into Hell and on the third day rose again and ascended into Heaven."

In recent years "descended into Hell" has been changed to "descended to the dead." Not that truth changes, but that words do. Meanings shift over the years. Hell once meant Sheol, Hades, the regions of the dead, not the Hell of eternal damnation. Christ descended there to bring all to His glorious Kingdom, the good dead who knew not Christ, whose salvation could only come from Him, without whom entrance into Heaven was impossible. For, there is no salvation but in Jesus. The Scriptures tell us that God enlightens everyone who comes into the world. When that light is heeded, when people do the best they can with what they have, their life has integrity that is completed by Christ's coming to them to rescue them from the powers of darkness and the fruit of the Evil One. The ancients called it the "harrowing of Hell." Both words have different meaning today, but it was the despoiling Satan of his victims that was involved.

If Christ's passion, death and rising are living experiences of today, if the contemporary world is redeemed by Christ's Cross and His grace poured out in our time, through the continued presence of His saving death, then Christ continues to descend to the regions of the dead, or in the archaic text, to descend into Hell—then all the dead who have not known Christ, His Church, but have followed what they had, follow Christ into His Kingdom. Something that goes on now, just as salvation goes on now. Or in the text of another day, "Salvation is applied through the ages in Mass and sacrament."

This is a beautiful truth. His passion, death, and now His rising are living realities in our day, realities reaching into the world of the dead, even the unnumbered dead who never knew Christ. Our response, of course, contributes to the cause, since in grace we build the Kingdom with Christ and bring His work to completion.

Here time is lost in eternity as darkness is lost in light, and sin and death in the merciful redeeming love of the savior now to rise from the dead.

4 ~ Saints

Bernard I

There is no immortality like holiness. It is immortality carried to full term. By virtue of being human we are immortal. Through our faith in Christ that immortality loses any suggestion of whimsy and wonder and becomes instead a living reality, a vision of coming happiness.

When faith is weak and undeveloped, or not present at all, the desire for immortality is apt to express itself in ways that seem rather pathetic. People will want to be remembered. They hope their name is passed on to children. They hope—many of them—to make a name in the world, to go down in history. To have streets, squares, parks, towns, buildings, trust funds, schools and colleges carrying their name seems to them a splendid achievement. The question arises, of course, in any reflecting mind, what possible good can come to James Duke for having a university named for him. If he enjoys reward for his goodness, his name identifying it has no significance. Yet the name on the marker over our head, on the stone above us, or even on an impressive monument, does give witness to the longing to live, to find in being remembered some assurance of it.

Is Saint Bernard happier because a breed of dog is named for him? Actually, the famous St. Bernard dog gets its name from the Hospice of St. Bernard of Menthon in the Swiss Alps, not for St. Bernard of Clairvaux. But how many know who St. Bernard of Clairvaux is? Does it matter if they know? Yes, it does matter. We can leave good after us that will nourish those who follow. Countless thousands do so in works of art, writing of every kind, bridges, public services, roads, highways, and all that makes civilized life possible: heat, light, water, transport, communication. We live after us in our successes in medicine, music, learning, and so much more. This is an immortality, and it is obviously good.

But true immortality is eternal life with God. Next to that, being remembered some way on earth is modest indeed. For all that, being remembered does nothing for those who are remembered. Is Diesel better off because every diesel engine is named for him?

Holiness moves the whole consideration onto another level, for through holiness we became a specific participant in the community of saints. In prayer, in grace, I can reach them, and they can reach me, in Christ. This community of love of the saints in Heaven, the faithful on earth, and the suffering in Purgatory is a true communion in love. Here remembering and being remembered is not idle or meaningless. It is love, and love is always dynamic.

God is remembered in all He left behind in creation and in sustaining that creation. We read God everywhere and in everything. If we do not, then we are blind indeed—the same blindness that afflicts those who fancy that the works they leave after them assure their immortality. They do nothing of the sort. We do not need to make ourselves immortal. We already are.

We need to acknowledge it, and that acknowledgment is an act of faith. One works, then, to attest to that immortality, as the universe attests to God. God is immortal without His works, and so are we.

As human, as Christ, as monk, we give witness by faith to human immortality. We make explicit what is often implicit, or implied. We make certain what is often nebulous, and this in the face of a materialistic world of thin faith, or no faith at all. We do so not in condemnation, but in mercy, in compassion, in intercession.

We remember St. Bernard as an historic figure who was of great significance and still is. He is among the immortals. He left a body of writing and a tradition in the Cistercian Order which immortalizes him in yet another way. He lives on and is an influence in a world he left nine hundred years ago. Most of all he is immortal by holiness, and as a saint we are in communion with, and he with us. This is more than mere remembering. This is love which is as real as the love of God because it is love rooted in God, a work of grace and a bonding union which is forever. We are not blind moles or hooded bats or barn-owls, but immortals destined for the Kingdom of God through Christ our Lord.

Joseph

At the end of Lauds and Vespers, after we make our petitions, we close with a commendation to the Virgin Mary when ends with a superb note, "We ask your prayers for these people and for all the world." At first one is not sure of one's hearing: "All the world?" It does seem a bit bold. No wonder Protestants gasp a bit at our estimate of the Virgin's powers. Who does she think she is? Or better, what do you try to make of her?

We might be very casual about it. Make nothing of it. She is a Christian and that alone makes her a participant in the world's redemption. In her case, the participation was considerably more than it is for most.

In prayer we enter into the mystery of Christ's splendid dream—the salvation of the world. He chose to do that with our help, our prayers are one with the prayer of the Son of God Almighty. This may be thought to be a powerful combination. If that is true of the Blessed Virgin—and it is—it is true of every Christian, and in a special way, of St. Joseph.

We were a way along in Christian history before devotion to St. Joseph became conspicuous. The Crusaders had a feeling for him and built a church in his honor at Nazareth. The Franciscans favored him and managed to have a feast of St. Joseph for all the Church through the Franciscan Sixtus IV. Patron of the Whole Church was a title that Pius IX gave him in 1870.

It is the vision of such a title that can stimulate our faith. Commending the whole world to the prayer of Mary seems a bit pretentious. Giving the whole Church over to the care of St. Joseph may seem little less.

Unless, of course, it occurs to you that your prayer ought to be no less Catholic. All our prayers are plural. We exclude none. We include all. We want none to go to Hell. We would have all saved. It is healthy to keep such a vision bright, to keep our piety generous. This is not to take on airs and assume a capacity we do not have, so much as a calling of faith to what we are in union with Jesus Christ, Son of God.

It is Christ who makes Mary what she is. It is Christ who made Joseph glorious. He who headed the Holy Family, spouse of the Virgin, foster father to the very Son of God, by right entered into a special bonding for all who are Christ's. Who had God's Son in his care can quite possibly look after His Church.

The odd thing is that in the praise of Mary and the glory of Joseph, we somehow come to sense what it means to be a Christian, that our priesthood in Jesus involves us in a great dream of the Lord's. Our prayer becomes an essential aspect of the dream's fulfillment. There ought to be no false diffidence and hesitancy in our role. It is not so much obligation as opportunity. Who can guess the power of prayer or measure it? Or to put it more blandly, what have you to lose in boldness in your prayer? Join the Virgin in prayer for the whole world, be one with St. Joseph in prayer for the Church.

There are trends, moods, attitudes, that seem to sweep through people. They are very mysterious and are difficult to explain. They are very real. They may be low level and involve nothing deeper than fashion, taste, and modishness. The commercial world pays a great deal of attention to such. They track down favor for a certain style, trace its movement, capitalize on it. The vast world of advertising is an endeavor to capture this mysterious power, often carried to terms that seem outrageous. Kraft Foods will spend eleven million next year pushing Kool-Aid, sugar water. It seems a bit pathetic.

Movements, trends, and tastes, also move in the world of the spirit. Many of them are evil, or questionable, or harmful. They sweep through a generation with great power, and seem independent of any identifiable source. But there are also good trends, holy movements, spiritualities of profound influence.

It is here that we enter the mysterious realms of prayer. We are often hesitant to think in terms of evil spirits and good spirits. Yet, who knows? We know so little. Fifty years ago seminaries were full and great numbers came to Gethsemani. Sisters and brothers and priests were abundant. Today houses are empty, priests and sisters are in short numbers, and motherhouses are vacant or used as conference centers.

Why? We don't know why. Europe seems to have abandoned the faith, but even that we are not sure of. If much in our land brings tears, there is also much to rejoice over. It seems impossible to have any real understanding. We are overwhelmed with data, surveys, and studies. We predict the worst and the best and are at a loss.

It is good to see all of this in a setting of prayer, prayer offered and prayer answered. The feast of St. Joseph should challenge us to make our Eucharist, our psalmody, our days, and our nights a share in the vision of Christ.

On March of 1872, one hundred twenty-five years ago, the monks wrote it down in stone in elegant Latin, here rendered in stiff English:

> To God, best and greatest, to the Blessed Virgin Mary,
> our Immaculate Lady,
> and to Blessed Joseph, who was chosen by the Trappist Monastery
> of Gethsemani,
> as patron, protector, defender,
> that day by day
> there may be an increase in the life,
> the merit, and
> the numbers of the brethren,
> and that those who seek God
> may never grow less in all that is good.
> Let this stone be an everlasting monument to all that.

Mary

This was in the paper recently:

"Romantics seeking to live happily ever after can now design their own ultimate Disney storybook wedding at Walt Disney World. The hotel is arranging all-inclusive weddings with themed balls, glass coach rides, a ceremony with a castle back-drop, Disney characters at the reception, Alice-in-Wonderland bridesmaid teas, and Pleasure Island pre-wedding parties. If live action themes are not magical enough, couples can choose a wedding based on Cinderella, Fantasia, or Beauty and the Beast."

So the Travel Section reports. Very nice. Americans and others go on pilgrimages as did our fathers before us. They go to Disneyland and Disneyworld. Appropriately enough. It is a kind of a cult of the mouse, and it's fitting that couples seek to be married there. A Disneyland memorial cemetery cannot be far off!

There is more pathos in this than humor. Effort to express something out of this world to give character to a human experience is old and valid. To be reduced by a faithless culture to doing so by nothing better than a fairy tale can only be the ultimate sadness.

The fairy tale was meant to be a bridge to the land of faith. By dint of imaginative story-telling involving the fantastic and the unreal, one is prepared to move beyond simple reason and reliance on rationality to the world of faith in the ostensibly unbelievable. Fairy tales, for all of their out-of-this-world character, always convey a message, a lesson, and often enough a hard lesson, a bitter truth. The happy ending is not characteristic. Dealing with darkness and evil is, so the preparation is sound.

We deal here with truths for which we might be well prepared through a childhood enriched by a full experience of fairy tales. The Cistercian order, this house and all monasteries of the Order are dedicated to the Holy Mother of God. Specifically, the high altar of this church is dedicated to her Assumption which we celebrate today.

The Assumption is a teaching that goes back to our roots as believers, even if it was precisely declared only in our own times. Just as this church being officially a basilica ties us to the most ancient churches of Christendom and so declares emphatically where we come from, what our roots are, so we believe in the Assumption because we are Catholic, not because it was declared dogma by Pope Pius XII in 1950. We are nothing if not historical.

We can understand the fact only if we see it in context, that is, the wholeness of the mystery of Christ. Central to this mystery, just as the Mass is central to our celebration of it, is the passion/death/rising of Jesus Christ.

Jesus is ours by way of a woman. The woman's name is Mary. By virtue of what she was called to be, she was conceived without sin. That is Part I. Part II is that she conceived of the Holy Spirit and became by the fact the mother of Jesus Christ, son of God. Part III is that Christ was born of her nine months later in the nativity of God on earth. Part IV is the climax of her Assumption into heaven which is our joy to celebrate today. They are all of a piece, all parts of a whole that necessarily go together. They are all essential.

They have a fairy tale quality. That is, are in some ways incredible; in other ways, essential to the faith story.

When we move into this world of faith, we are at once fundamentally historical—we deal with facts—and essentially transcendental That is the fairy-tale quality.

If we see Christ and His passion/death/rising as the focus, we can see Mary as the first great ring of glory around the Godhead. The four moons of that glorious rainbow are her conception, her conceiving, her giving birth, and her joyous assumption. These mysteries are resplendent in the glory of God and after them follow the unending ranks of the redeemed, stretching into infinity, bright with God's splendor. "Eye has not seen, ear has not heard...."

One would need more than a human imagination to picture heaven, yet in faith we can get some notion of what is to come. All of it began here on earth, in time. All the people are real. They lived. All the events are historical, they happened. If it all surpasses any fairy tale in splendor, it all surpasses fairy tales for being history.

As a people of God, we are wed to the Lord in undying love. We will one day be with Him, body and soul. The Mother of Christ, and so our mother, is already there, promise and guarantee of the fact, for which God is praised.

Our Lady of Guadalupe

 We are pleased to honor Our Lady of Guadalupe, no stranger to us. She is much loved here. We are glad she has come, now in this holy season, now in time of need.

She loves the poor and the oppressed. Her visit to Guadalupe, only forty years after Columbus came to this part of the world, was dramatic, memorable, and beautiful. Whether it was effective, God alone knows. If despite her coming the treatment of the Indians continued to be dismal, one can only ask, what if she had not come?

Her appeal today is the same. Yankees have no great love for her or for Latins, let alone Indians. North American lack of love for blacks is well known. There are tensions among people old among us, and now new. In all parts of the world people hate and fight because they are different. Live among them; you do not need to read the newspaper to find out these things.

So she comes for Jesus' sake, for love's sake, the more so now at Christmas. Let her visit among us be memorable. Treat someone better today than yesterday because she came.

Our Lady of Guadalupe is a standing reproach to us Europeans, which most of us are. She passed us up in favor of an Aztec Indian when she came to visit America. She is kindly, she is courteous, but she is not pleased with sin. So we ask her pardon, her prayers, and may she please accept our thanks for her coming.

John the Baptist

The Catholic cult of the saints is a bit more than an annual calling to mind of the holy, each properly annotated and brought out for display on the appropriate day, like the newspaper will feature an article or two on Lincoln or Washington or whomever when their dates turn up.

Our approach would be more in the nature of a family reunion, and the honored guest would be a living presence. We are in communion with the saints. They are part of the Church as we are, and we are in touch. All of us—Church militant, Church suffering, Church Triumphant in Heaven—are united in the love of God and one another.

The whole Christian thing has a sort of timelessness which at once removes it from the confines of time and yet essentially unites it with every moment of time. The Passion, Death, and Rising, are not only historical events, they are mystical events which step out of time and so are present in all time.

We do not merely read the Scriptures, we do them. In the mystical dimension that is essential to our Faith we participate in the most significant events of history. It is far more than recall, than memory or recollection. The Church lives, and lives always, not merely in time past.

So our celebration of John the Baptist is no mere pausing in a busy week to think of him and his life and work and reflect on it. John is not gone. John lives. His ministry continues. He is martyred in new Johns and new Johns give testimony to Jesus, "Behold, the Lamb of God!"

Fascination with the Baptist continues. His name is still a most popular name. He is at once Old Testament and New. He is a son of the desert, a devotee of silence and solitude, whose preaching infuriated because it exposed the follies of his time and people.

He continues. His scorn is poured out on our new breed of millionaires. While workers' pay stagnates and declines, this greedy brood of vipers cares not. The president of Ford, who earns eight million a year, had to issue a recall to eight million Fords for defective and hazardous equipment. We, one of the richest nations in the world, have a high poverty rate for children, one out of five below the poverty line. We are the stingiest of major nations in helping other less developed lands. We have five million citizens behind bars or on probation or parole. Half of our marriages collapse. Abortion destroys life with savage abandon. John's voice is heard. He may as well bay at the moon and scream in the night for the good it does. No matter! His ministry continues and very much matters. Do not be too sure it is not heard.

We are involved in it, for Christianity is not a memory trip, a cult of the past. It has no past. It is timeless. It all goes on now. We are present and make a response. We are not permitted merely to stand by to watch, wringing our hands at the state of things, hastening to tell the latest bad news to the next person we meet.

John was born as summer begins. It is actually the beginning of winter, for now the days grow shorter, the nights longer, and only in the deeps of that deep darkness is Christ the Light born. John points him out.

Our call, then, is to live John by an honesty of vision which is not deceived by the corruption of our times, however elegant. Not in bitterness, but in joy does our Faith in hope trust. In the darkness of the night we retreat into the desert of the heart and there nurture the light that redeems the world.

The New Eve

This sermon was preached by Father Matthew on the Golden Jubilee of his ordination.

God's heart was broken over His first human family. He was grievously disappointed that His gifts were so misused that they took steps that led only to unhappiness for them and all who were to follow.

God determined that He would find some way to mend the harm done, to set things right again, and would do so both with the help of His children and without violating their freedom and their integrity, their persons.

So He dreamed of His Son entering the human family and His doing so by way of a human mother, a woman. He knew what would happen to His Son at the hands of men and yet was determined to make of that very tragedy the healing of the wounded who did it.

Hence Mary. Born beautiful by virtue of her Son's coming sacrifice, perfectly lovely, not touched with evil, born as we were all meant to be born, and so first fruit of her Son's redeeming love.

She became virginal mother of the Son of God, made fruitful by the Holy Spirit, who sowed the seed of the Divine in her. He thus sanctified anew and forever the fertility of woman in the act of generation, the glory of humankind for participation in creating eternal life. In terms of carnal union she remained a virgin. In terms of God's union with her she became mother of the Son of God.

So, she became a new Eve, mother of all the living in Christ, remaining a virgin because our first call is to union with God. Because God would have us all involved in His saving work, she became mother of sorrows, receiving at the foot of the cross the body of her Son done to death by sinners, joining Him in His redemptive prayer for universal healing. She then witnessed His rising in glory, triumphant over sin and death, returning humankind to its original state, and more, through their union with Him for an eternal destiny.

The Mother of Christ, when her time had come, relived the original dream of God and was assumed into Heaven when life on earth was done. The original plan was at last fulfilled. Mary recovers human glory through her Son, becoming forever the mother of the redeemed for all and for all time.

So today in a world of so much darkness and ugliness, we give witness to the light, to the joy of God in the glory of Mary. The original dream has at last come true, the original sin has been undone. We believe all this, enter into all of it, indeed participate in it all.

I, for one, do so with special joy and great gratitude, since the hands of a bishop were laid upon me fifty years ago today to mark me and make me a priest of God. I pray you thank God with me and for me.

The Martyrs of Holland

LUKE 24:35–48

In the *New York Times* for December 25, 1941, a front page story carried the headline, "Pope Condemns Persecutions." The newspaper claimed in an editorial that day, "The voice of Pius XII is a lonely voice in the silence and darkness of Europe. He is about the only ruler left on the continent of Europe who dares raise his voice at all. The Pope squarely sets himself against Hitlerism. This Christmas, more than ever, the Pope is a lonely voice."

When Pius XII died, Mrs. Golda Meir, Israel's Minister of Foreign Affairs, said at the United Nations, "We share the grief of the world over the death of his holiness Pius XII. During a generation of wars and dissensions, he affirmed the high ideals of peace and compassion. During the ten years of Nazi terror, when our people went through the horrors of martyrdom, the Pope raised his voice to condemn the persecutors and to commiserate with their victims. The life of our time has been enriched by a voice which expressed the great moral truths about the tumult of daily conflicts. We grieve over the loss of a great defender of peace."

One presumes Golda Meir knew what she was talking about. Many commentators on Pius XII today do not.

Not many of us seem to know that the savage hand of Hitler reached also into Cistercian abbeys and left death in concentration camps a memorial of his visit.

It is hard to grasp the intensity of a persecution that would reach into abbeys of nuns and monks. It was well for the Dutch Bishops to protest vehemently the treatment their German invaders were giving the Dutch of Jewish extraction. Yet, the immediate response to that protest was to go further and retaliate, take even converts to the Faith who were Jewish, some three hundred of them. Hitler was a madman, and Pius XII knew that.

In the cemetery of the Cistercian Abbey of Tilburg, Holland, is a simple monument to Ignatius, Linus, and Nivard Lob who, in the year 1942, "perished in the name of Christ in the concentration camp of Auschwitz." The remarkable thing about the Lob brothers was that they had three sisters who were also Cistercians, and two of the three sisters also perished in the Nazi persecution of the Jews, as did a younger brother named Hans who had remained in the world.

Ludwig Hans Lob, father of the family, was a German-born Jew. He was for a time interested in Marxism, but was later attracted to Catholicism through reading the works of Mercier. Just before his marriage in 1906, he and his Jewish fiancée were baptized into the Catholic Church. They migrated to Holland.

The Lobs, though not wealthy, were a very hospitable family, and Mrs. Lob especially was very popular in their town and district. In due course eight children were born to the family between 1908 and 1918. George, the eldest, a joyous and exuberant youth, entered the Cistercian Abbey of Tilburg, taking the name Ignatius. He was later followed by Robert who became Linus and by the more serious Ernst who took the name Nivard.

Meanwhile, the girls also followed the call to religion. Lina, the eldest, full of motherly solicitude and good humor, became Sister Hedwige. Door and Weis, neither of them very strong physically, took the names of Therese and Veronica. All were in the Cistercian convent of Berkel. Only one son and daughter, Hans and Paula, now remained with their parents. In due course both father and mother died saintly deaths.

Then came World War II and the Nazi invasion of Holland. The Dutch bishops protested against the atrocities committed against the Jews. By way of public reprisal, the Nazis decided to round up all Jews of Catholic faith.

Early on Sunday morning, August 2, 1942, as the nuns of Berkel were singing the Night Office, the SS men arrived at the convent and asked for the three sisters. They left choir, received Holy Communion from the Chaplain and went to the waiting police car. Sister Veronica, who was seriously ill with tuberculosis, was allowed to return to the convent. The police then drove to Tilburg Abbey some miles away and asked for the brothers. Fathers Ignatius and Linus were able to say Mass, and then with Brother Nivard, who was a laybrother, joined their sisters, whom they had not seen for a number of years, in the police car.

In all, about three hundred Catholic Jews were arrested, including the famous Carmelite, Edith Stein. They were taken to the infamous Auschwitz camp in Poland. A captured Nazi document notes the deaths of the Lob brothers and sisters in August and September of 1942.

Sister Veronica, who was ill with tuberculosis, was later arrested, but again released. She died in Berkel convent in 1944. Hans, the youngest, was sent to Germany for forced labor, had his feet frozen later when traveling in an open truck, and died in 1945 in Buchenwald. The youngest girl, Paula, escaped arrest as she found shelter with a charitable family in Nymegen. She was the only surviving member of the family.

When the war was over and the horrors of Hitler's regime were exposed, there was, of course, much anguish. Some may have turned to the Pope and said in effect, "You should have spoken louder!" He, in turn, might well have been bitter and replied, "And where were you? You knew. You said nothing. I am fortunate if Catholics listen to me and obey me. Many do not. Christians may give me a hearing. They may not. But to expect a madman to obey is a bit much. And he can retaliate by doing worse. But I spoke, and he heard me and did as he liked."

In today's Gospel passage there is a very remarkable word from Jesus. Standing with them in the upper room, He asks, "Have you anything to eat?" They must have been embarrassed, humiliated, that they had not offered him hospitality. On the shore of the lake in the early morning fog, He called out to them over the water, "Have you any fish?"

The food that Jesus asks of us is our faith in Him. The whole mystical body of Christ is nourished by obedient faith in Him. The Church grows and progresses in vigorous health when we offer Him the bread of faith, the fish of our committed life.

To withhold such food, such fish, is to impoverish the Church and humankind, expose us to sickness and evil of every sort, let loose among us demons and evil powers that will wreak havoc among us.

"Have you anything to eat?" We do indeed. "Have you any fish?" We have. And he says, "Bring Me some."

George[1]

Some years ago, thirty-four to be exact, about the time George Devine was with the summer symphony in Ravinia Park north of Chicago, I had a dream. I had come here, mid-life, from an active world, somewhat bruised by years and sin, to a quiet life among strangers who did not speak a language I knew. Though I never doubted that what I had done was good and right, it was nonetheless difficult. In the midst of that stress and anguish, I had a dream. It involved a professor of philosophy at the seminary where I was trained, author of a series of Latin texts, small, intense, very ascetical, much the model of holiness as conceived at the time. He came in a dream, this vision of my past, and in full front face, large and clear. He pointed his finger at me and said with great intensity, "What you are doing is a very beautiful thing." I walked in the strength of the vision many days.

Now comes a man, burdened with years, but not with sin, rather with infirmities, about to make an even more momentous step. It is no less a marvel of grace. How comes it that saved by the purification of suffering, a man in whom hearing has long since ceased to function normally, can hear so clearly the voice of God? How comes it that a man whose sight has long since wearied of further service, can have such a sharp vision of truth? How comes it that a man no longer able to get about as he once could, but is dependent on others to go anywhere, can with alacrity follow the call of the Lord with speed and grace? How comes it that a man once graced with gifts of music of eminent quality,

---

[1] George Devine, a professional musician, dear friend of one of the monks, was received into the Catholic Church late in life, nearly blind, long retired. The reception was at the Abbey, and these remarks were made at the event.

now but a memory, should in such poverty know the shrewdness of the poor and where real wealth and beauty lay?

I say, we are witness to God at work. How comes a man who has known suffering and sorrow, loneliness and pain, the caprice of human existence, the frustration of being helpless and alone, to know a grace so hidden and so profound—a grace unseen by most, not much acknowledged and reckoned with, precious and beautiful beyond telling: full communion with Christ and Peter. One can only marvel.

One can only say with great emphasis and with great gratitude to God, "George Devine, what you are doing is a very beautiful thing!"

May the beauty live forever and be eternal joy to you, to angels, and to people.

Bernard II

Old families relish memories of past glory in their lineage. Current members make much of history and somehow give the impression that they share eminence if only by inheritance. Yet, after all, my ancestors are as ancient as yours. What mine did probably matters as little to me as what yours did to you.

But it is not quite that simple. We do inherit and we do pass on qualities and characteristics. If our sins are passed on to the next generation, so are our virtues. There are families of noble tradition like the Morgenthaus, a distinguished New York Jewish family of means and position whose patrician code disdains show and self-serving and is committed to high moral purpose in public service.

So there is a point to pride in being Irish and an inheritor of the Celtic charism. There is honor in being Catholic and a member of Christ. We do sense glory in being Benedictine and in living a tradition fourteen hundred years old. So too we share a certain aura in being Cistercian, members of an Order over nine hundred years old, who live in a house where the praise of God has been chanted seven times a day for over one hundred and fifty years.

To be sure, our glory in all the above is as much gratitude to God as anything else for reason of our having had so little to do with it. Even the little we did do seems so modest that we would hesitate to talk about it for sheer shame. Comparing what you have and what I have, what connections are mine and what yours, is a risky business.

St. Bernard prepared for the monastic life one who was to become Pope Eugene III. Bernard was a great figure in the Council of Etampes, was consulted by William of Aquitaine, by the Duchess of Lorraine, by the Countess of Britanny, by Henry, son of the King of France, by Peter, son of the King of Portugal, by Louis VI, by Louis VII, by emperprs

Conrad and Lothaire, and by the abbot of St. Denis. He silenced Abelard at the Council of Laon, overwhelmed Arnold of Brescia and Peter de Bruys, preached a Crusade against Islam, and founded in passing one hundred sixty monasteries. He died this day in 1153 at sixty-two years. He left a treasure of writing that continues to nourish monks and others even today, homilies preached to his monks at Clairvaux.

A splendid achievement by any standard. To be sure, the record seems less impressive, say, beside that of John Paul II, who perhaps sees more significant people in a month that Bernard did in a lifetime, whose own journeys make Bernard's travels across Europe seems slight excursions.

Yet, take care. You are not judged by his time, but by yours. What John Paul does is what John Paul will be judged for. You and I will not be questioned on Citeaux and Clairvaux, but on Gethsemani; not on the twelfth century, but this one. It is not given to Bernard to walk in our cloister, nor to us in his.

But we love the Lord he loved. Here is where we meet. Here all differences vanish. We center on what makes us who we are and what we are. So Bernard could stand at this altar and break the Bread and share the Cup. He could hear the Rule read, heed the abbot, sing in choir.

Christ is really all that matters. Anything else is negotiable, of limited significance.

The glory of Biltmore looks a bit foolish today, if it didn't the day the Vanderbilts built it. Hearst's San Simeon is even more absurd, as significant as Disneyland.

This is not to disparage or belittle, but to put in perspective. Human life is not diminished by an immortal reference, but it is made ridiculous when that reference is lost. All ridicule soon turns to hate and hate to violence. You deny immortality at your own risk.

Hence a feast like today's is once again to touch base, to connect once more. It is to take the long view, not from the bottom of the valley, but high on the slope where splendid vistas come into sight.

You are gifted. Use your gifts. Spend them freely and generously, but not for gain of any kind. To be the most impressive monk in the monastery has a certain absurdity about it when you think it means much, not to say being least of all. What has that to do with anything?

Christ, Son of the living God is in love with me, and I with Him. Nothing, anywhere, anytime, here and for all eternity, can mean more than that, for you, for me, for all of us. Here is our glory, and Bernard's.

Taking up the Cross

Steve Redgrave is 34, is 6'5", weights 225 pounds, and for the last eighteen years has devoted himself to rowing and only that. A six hour workout each day, seven days a week, for some ten races a year, 6½ minutes each. He ends up being a world's top rower, five Olympic medals if he won at Atlanta, which he was predicted to do. Now he resigns, with no idea what he will do with the rest of his life.

He is a classic case of commitment, dedication, and discipline. It is a case of incredible tenacity, for rowing is unique in that it is a fast-start sport. You row at top speed instantly. The result is the highest level of lactic acid in the muscles and excruciating pain. Eighty percent of rowing is learning to cope with pain.

How is it then, that we who seek love assume that somehow it should not be too difficult in the grace of God, require no great endeavor, need no demanding discipline? That is what we seem to do. Yet, after all, love is the greatest of arts, is a world away and beyond athletics, skills of whatever kind, prowess and competence in whatever field. It is the art of arts, and the love of God as art is sanctity. There is no greater good on earth or in heaven. It is literally a life-time work. We cannot assume then that it is easily come by. Not when He says things like, "Take up My cross. Who would save his life will lose it. Let a person deny self and follow Me. What profit is it to gain a world and lose one's soul?"

In the face of which dodges are in order, that is to say, short-cuts, quick routes, and easy answers. This is a delusion and a trap. This is marsh. Quagmire. Here is the Dismal Swamp of Carolina transferred to Redfield spirituality and talk of synchronicity, coincidence, apotheosis, energy fields, universal sacredness, mystical illumination, higher consciousness, transcendent love. And the best part: without pain and effort. There is no rule of life, no laws, no commandments, no obligations, no confrontation with evil, no repentance, no penance. It is ethics-free and morals free, this fantasy world. Above all, no institution, least of all, God forbid, a patriarchal one.

People buy into it, pay for it, eat it up. So Augustine did and got so tangled he was years breaking free.

Thus it is with today's Catholics, too, who, God knows, need law and rule, need penitence and penance, need authority and direction, need sacrament and Word, need absolution and anointing, need prayer.

On all of which many turn their backs. Everybody knows going to Sunday mass is no longer a universally accepted tradition. Among Christians, Catholics rate very poorly in financial Church support—always revealing. They do not differ that much from other Americans in many attitudes and practices in the world of marriage. That's why President Clinton had a Catholic woman speak for abortions. She is not unusual and he knows that.

This sad picture means not mere disenchantment with the Church, but covert and overt hostility. Disagreement. And tantamount if not actual departure. Talk of vocations in such a setting is a bit naïve.

It is obvious that such are not about to turn to a disciplined unselfish life in which the Cross is a basic theme, the acceptance of suffering a dimension of Christian reality.

All of which is a bit irrelevant for monks. Neo-gnosticism is not an issue we cope with. But the mood is in the air, the attitude spreads. We are touched by a tainted milieu.

Hence it is not without point to note the heroic sacrifice men and women will make to attain excellence in some profession—from athletics, to dance, to music, medicine, how many fields. This should spur us on, remind us of God's gift to us, how necessary a generous response.

This is said by way of encouragement to carry on in so good a work, a work often without much tangible result. Surely there is no professional in whatever field from piano to shot-put who does not at times sense defeat, failure, lack of progress, no tangible reward for so much effort; not reward really, but response, growth, a sense of achieving something? And still they carry on. Think sometimes of the man who gave eighteen years to rigorous training for perfection in rowing, a perfection that won him five gold Olympic medals. So much for so little.

We do so little for so much that we may feel shame. Called to the service of God in a most beautiful life, with a promise of Eternal Life to follow. Even if we know a lactic acid of our own, we carry on in God's generous grace. So, hopefully, we encourage the faithful to deep love for God, for Christ, for the Church—the love that is truly one's life work, the work of a lifetime.

The Call to Extravagance

 ## MARK 12:38–44

Father Solanus Casey was a Capuchin. He was born in Detroit in 1870 and died there in 1957 at age eighty-six. He was ordained in 1904, but with a strict proviso: he was never the preach, never the hear confessions, never to teach. He was what was called a "Mass priest." He served as a porter in a New York friary for twenty years, served thirty years as porter in a friary in Detroit. He was richly endowed with the Holy Spirit, he could read souls, though intellectually he was poor. There were 10,000 people at his funeral. He is to be canonized as a true man of God. He gave all he had.

There are about 50,000 priests in this country and about 100,000 sisters. We Cistercians of this branch number about five hundred here: four hundred monks, one hundred nuns. But we give what we have. Even our dead are few. We have some two hundred in our graveyard. To be sure, many went onto daughter houses. But the number is modest. Nazareth has maybe two thousand, only a few decades older. Yet, however, few ours be, they gave all.

Like the woman in the gospel today. Jesus does not call it the widow's mite. We do. He praised her because she gave all. In a subsistence community, one can manage with little cash. It was all she had. She gave it to the Church, all of it.

It was the wealthy who gave the mite. We should call the story the rich person's mite. To be sure, they were generous. They had means and they shared it. Praiseworthy enough. But what they did could not hold a candle to what the widow did. She was munificent on a shoe-string.

Then why make comparisons? They can be odious. Margaret Truman could sing, had a pleasant voice, was trained. But in comparison with quality professionals, she did not make it. But she gave what she had.

So why compare, then? Probably because that's what the disciples were doing. They perhaps smiled or made disparaging remarks about the widow and her gift. Christ frequently took up passing comments, showing that even by their own standards the disciples did not make sense. "Why choose the best seat? You make be asked to move lower. Even by your own standards you lack insight." No one became honorable by playing the part, looking important, being prominent. That is no route to honor. Even by your own logic, you do not pass. It's the way of the world, though. Big people drive big cars.

We are called to be big. Not in the way of the world, but in the way of the widow—extravagant—in the way of the widow gathering sticks, bringing water to Elijah and bread, though she uses the last of what little she has for him. Extravagant woman. Like the poor Jesus Who stripped Himself of glory to become poor for our sake that He might lead us to glory and eternal riches in Him. Extravagant!

So the call is to extravagance, not prudence; munificence, not shrewd calculation. We can do it once in a while. Doing it once in a while makes it possible to do it once and for all when we make a leap of faith and accept Jesus wholly and His Church—His Spouse, His Bride, His Body. It is an extravagance we never regret and never renege on. This and this alone makes life worth living. The two widows were on to something. One hopes we are. And if we are, there is no hiding it. If you're stingy, you never got the message. No one who has drunk the wine of extravagance will ever stoop to stinginess on anything. Total gift brings total freedom.

The Shepherd

MARK 6:30–34

If I understood aright, the Marlboro Man will soon disappear from the American scene. At least that is the plan. The Marlboro Man is undoubtedly a work of advertising genius, for the cowboy is a major icon of our national life, heavy with many layers of meaning. He has nothing to do with cigarettes, but by dint of unrelenting association, a tobacco company was able to promote a brand with phenomenal success. They might have chosen any one of many: the sailor, the marine, the fireman, the lobster fisherman, the prairie farmer—all can be rendered in classic form. But the cowboy is exceptional and known over all the world, now forever associated with Marlboro country.

The shepherd is an older symbol and far more widespread, usually with sheep rather than cattle or horses. It runs as a constant through the Scriptures and is with us to this day. Old Testament David proved his mettle in killing a lion and a bear while guarding his flock. Yahweh is Israel's shepherd and led His people out of Egypt. Poor, negligent shepherds are rebuked and shown as poor examples to be avoided. God promises His people a good shepherd who will lead His people. Best of all, Christ applied the term to Himself, as one who leads His flock, seeks out the lost, gives His life for His sheep. In the service of His people, shepherds are bidden to be generous, unselfish, and dedicated. "Feed My lambs. Feed My sheep."

Even though we are remote from sheep, from shepherds, our bishops still carry the shepherd's crook, as does every abbot and abbess. The term is aptly applied to those who would serve others: Good Shepherd Sisters. House of the Good Shepherd, Good Shepherd Hospital.

There are those who resent being called sheep or who do not relish

124

being a flock cared for and watched over. I do not know as one should make too much of that. Some people are born resentful. For all that, one need not drive the metaphor into the ground. Most can see the points of the comparison, else the usage would long since have been dropped.

The image has great power. There is some reason for seeing people as sheep: lost, confused, mixed up, wandering, in grave danger. Like all sheep, they look for greener pastures, but alas for their choices. Unhappy sheep are everywhere and often enough unhappy by their own doing.

So it is good to keep love for Peter warm, the Good Shepherd Christ appointed to guard His Church. It is fitting to love your bishop, your abbot, your pastor. It is a very shrewd response to reality. We can all be as innocent and as naïve as any lamb, taken in by the latest fashion, wandering far from truth in pursuit of fables.

It is very dangerous to make general statements. Perhaps it could be ventured that though the Spirit of God is patently at work in the world and with astonishing results, there is a certain disenchantment with the Church and with Church teaching today here and everywhere. Disenchantment with shepherds is a perilous attitude for sheep. It may be characteristic of them. Maybe we are more like sheep than we care to admit.

I believe the answer is prayer. Pray for your shepherd. That will help him and will surely help his flock.

I do consider that a certain compassion for Christ the Good Shepherd is called for. See what humankind has done to His Church, His fold under one shepherd. What a mess. What a heartbreak. What further stimulus do we need to pray for a good Shepherd who will lead His flock together again, that all will recognize His voice and heed it.

I went twelve years to public schools. They were more religious then than now. We prayed the Our Father every day, sang a hymn, read some Scripture, and said the Twenty-third Psalm. Here it is in the King James Version:

> The Lord is my Shepherd. I shall not want.
> He maketh me to lie down in green pastures.
> He leadeth me beside the still waters.
> He restoreth my soul.
> He leadeth me in the paths of righteousness
>   for His name's sake.

Yea, tho I walk through the valley of the shadow of death,
    I will fear no evil
For thou art with me.
Thy rod and thy staff they comfort me.
Thou preparest a table before me
in the presence of mine enemies.
Thou anointest my head with oil. My cup overflows.
Surely goodness and mercy shall follow me,
    all the days of my life,
And I will dwell in the house of the Lord forever.

Love in Depth[1]

On the thirtieth anniversary of the death of Thomas Merton

It was Tuesday, the second week of Advent and we were at dinner, at noon, that is, eating our beans and rice, lettuce salad, preceded by pea soup and followed by an apple for desert. The reader that week was Father Timothy Kelly, and the book was the life of Teilhard de Chardin. It was the 10th of December. The abbot was Father Flavian Burns. At the end of the meal instead of ringing the bell—so we knew something was up—he went to the reader's desk, signed him to stop, picked up the microphone, and said:

"Brothers, I have sad news for you. Fr. Louis died in Bangkok. That is all I know. I'll let you know more when I learn it."

He then said the closing meal prayers and life went on as usual. And forever different.

* * *

As you may know, there is currently a phenomenal growth in church building, last year more than in any year in the last three decades. Mostly in the south and southwest. One major project: a new cathedral in Los Angeles. Not all is happiness, however. One contractor after handling a four-year parish renovation vowed he'd never do a church again. The plans were changed more often than the wind, he said. His architects warned him: never again. Monks were like that. And they love to build. The library building, once the Brothers' novitiate, began as a shops' building. Plans were changed seven times, the Brothers said. Even one novice, and architect, had a hand: he suggested the third-floor balcony with the ten arches. The retreat house fared no better. So

[1] From *The Merton Seasonal*, vol. 24, 1 Spring 1999.

when it came to the church, the Brother in charge thought having an architect would avoid a disastrous committee production. And he so convinced the abbot.

The plans were submitted, lots of discussion, final agreement. Finished. No more input. But toward the end of the project, the monks did a monk thing, a human thing, suggested a change. An ugly scene resulted. At which point I happened to see Fr. Louis and mentioned to him: "Well, they've turned against Mr. Schickel." At once he turned in his swivel chair, took a slip of paper, put it into his Underwood and wrote the architect a note of thanks and commendation for his work. "Here," he said, "give this to him." It was not that liked the church—a matter of opinion—no. But he did not like dirty pool.

Instant assessment of a situation. Instant response. Total indifference to the consequences; to what others might think.

* * *

On a more serious level Maximillian Kolbe in a concentration camp lined up with the others while the officer sent every tenth one to the starvation block in reprisal for escaped prisoners. As he came down the line the choice fell on one who screamed in panic that he had a wife and children. At once Maximillian Kolbe spoke up: "Kommandant! Lass mir seinen platz nehmen!"— "Wenn sie wunschen!" ["Let me take his place!" — "If you wish."]

Had you been there, had I been there, we might have had a similar thought. "But I am a priest and they need me. Maybe I would break down and go to pieces. Anyway, I'm a monk and should ask the abbot first." By then, of course, it is too late and the opportunity gone.

Instant grasp of the situation.

Instant response.

Total indifference to the consequences.

Kolbe was not canonized for that act. That's what he did all the time. He lived that way. His last act was typical, not exceptional. It is sanctity of high order.

I dare say Merton lived the same way. As delicate as a wind chime to any breath of the Spirit.

* * *

You can get burned that way, of course. It can be humbling, humiliating, difficult. And in serious matters, it may have to be submitted to an abbot who may or may not assent to what the Spirit seems to be telling you.

True love in depth means death to the ego, means the emergence of a person possessed by God, and instrument of God. Here we have the genesis of the saint. It is not easy.

* * *

A man named Hal Edwards, a retired executive on the north shore of Chicago, fosters small prayer groups throughout the area. A Protestant, he was familiar with Merton's work, but no great fan or disciple. Digging a post hole in his back yard with a rented power tool, he struck and broke a 7,000-volt cable that fed the whole of Northbrook. The strike caused a great noise and a cloud of smoke, in the midst of which he had a clear moment of vision of Thomas Merton dead of electrocution.

When the power people arrived they could not believe he was still alive. "You're the third one this week: one is dead, one is dying in a hospital. You have no business being alive." "You a Catholic?" "Yes." "Well, I should tell you—I had a clear vision of Thomas Merton, the monk, when it happened." "Well, you'd better get to your knees and thank Thomas Merton that you're alive. And go see a doctor and get checked out." In Hal Edwards eyes, we deal with a miracle. He later came to the abbey for the first time and thanked Fr. Louis.

So Merton is patron of all who work with dangerous power lines? Maybe. Better say, he is patron of all who would dearly love God, who would go deep to search for his light and beauty, who would do his Will, whatever and whenever. In such an enterprise Merton is our friend and advocate. And protector. And guide.

For getting close to God is to get close to fire. And fire can burn. It is not that only those who love God are touched by fire, for all are, sooner or later. But to love God deeply and be totally given to Him, in perfect response to His love is to recognize whence comes the fire that makes love "a harsh and bitter thing."

It is not that Merton suffered more than most, so much as that he loved more, and more deeply. Therefore his engagement with God was more profound, his commitment more total, his abandonment more complete. In such a life the relation to God is superbly intimate, and no mortal living with such love can escape being burned. He was thus a perfect vehicle for God's work in the world: pure, empty, clean of self, and thus the medium of great good, then and still. The best way to honor him is to endeavor to follow him in love. He wrote well of himself in *The Seven Storey Mountain*:

> But you shall taste the pure solitude of My anguish and My poverty and I shall lead you into the high places of My joy and you shall die in Me and find all things in My mercy which has created you for this end, and brought you from Prades to Bermuda to St. Antonin to Oakham to London to Cambridge to Rome to New York to Columbia to Corpus Christi and St. Bonaventure to the Cistercian abbey of the poor men who labor in Gethsemani: that you may become the brother of God and learn to know the Christ of the burnt men. *Sit finis libri, non finis quaerendi.*[2]

End of the book and long later, end of the search. God bless him. Praise God. Amen.

---

[2]   From *The Seven Storey Mountain*, (NY: Harcourt Brace & Jovanovich, 1999), pg. 462.

5 ～ Ethics and Evil

Abortion:
A Personal Experience

The Archbishop has asked us to join him and his flock in prayer and penance for the nation over the sin of abortion. We respond. We will eat less today and pray a bit more, and think about deep things: the issues of life and death, birth and immortality.

It is, of course, a great sadness that so gross an evil as abortion should become entrenched among us, and among the Catholic flock, too. So great is the pressure of trend and fashion, spirits that move through the world subtly and powerfully.

It does not seem an appropriate concern of monks or nuns who live celibate lives. It isn't. But we were born. We come from a family. We remain part of a family, and we love. We love our land and our people. It does not rest well on the heart that so many would be deceived by this world, act so foreign to our nature, contradict reality in such a gross way.

It is not as if the Church invented love for life, or the Ten Commandments were imposed on us by some arbitrary God. Our faith is consonant with nature, rooted in it. The law is from within, not without.

How long does it take a people to discover what works and what doesn't work? That is to say, what is natural to us and what is not? Primitive peoples were thousands of years discovering what wears and what does not.

You cannot violate your nature and get by with it. Our stand is not judgmental. We do not preach the fires of Hell. We are much more here and now. But, go contrary to nature and you contradict reality. The consequences are enormous. It will not work. You cannot get away with it. It does not wear; it does not sell. You have been had when they tell you that it is normal and healthy, and above all, in your rights.

I can tell you a story that I have not told often. I once told it in a retreat to Lutherans in the Highlands of New Guinea, among strangers in a far away place.

My father was a good man, but he slept with a girl in the southwest once while on some engineering project, and he caught syphilis. My mother was outraged, indignant, angry, and hurt. A child was conceived. It was well on the way when she went to the parish priest and told him she was convinced the child was rotten, sick, bad. She would abort it. She asked his permission. He told her in clear terms she certainly could do no such thing. This is South Boston, Irish, 1915, when the cure for syphilis was probably bicarbonate of soda. She listened to the priest. The child was born, healthy and normal. I was the child.

What she had wanted to do with me haunted her the rest of her life.

She and my father are long dead. They are all gone. She never knew that I knew, for I discovered it by mere accident.

When I told her I was to be a priest, she took it hard, though I did not know till years later that she wanted to get rid of me.

She lived her life with what she almost did, and did not, thanks to Father Toomey. She never knew I knew, and I have not talked about it. But I am witness to the devastating damage of those who abort, who would abort. You will be a lifetime with it, so unnatural is it, so alien. We are overcome by darkness and murk when we lose sight of that.

We do not condemn, point the finger, or send to Hell. We rather pray. It is grace and light involved, not human passion.

We never talked of it, but I think she came to peace and grace in the end. The consequences of this evil are enormous for society. I knew even in the womb. The mother who survives knows, too. Our response to that is prayer rooted in mercy. Prayer rooted in mercy.

Mission

MATTHEW 22:15–21

This is world mission Sunday. Catholic and mission go together, since we are commissioned to go forth into all the world. Our prayer by nature is Catholic, that is to say, all-embracing. We live for the Kingdom and the salvation of all. Our prayers are plural and exclude none.

It begins in the heart, the center of love, for heart follows head, love follows knowledge, and leads to action in the service of the cross. You are a Catholic in contradiction if you do not live for all. The role you do is in the Providence of God.

The mode, the manner, the way, is peace. When Christ speaks of bringing the sword, of not coming for peace, He speaks of the spiritual war against the power of darkness and evil, the fight that continues to the end. But the weapons are prayer and goodness, non-violence, justice and mercy.

The Pharisees of Christ's day seemed to have caught the messianic fervor that was in the air at the time, an expectancy that led them to fashion the One who was to come according to their own designs. High on the list of the messianic agenda would be a free Israel, rid forever of the hated occupying Romans. But with Christ, their misgivings were early and evident.

In today's piece from the Gospel, they approach the Lord. Aware of their own ambivalence toward Him, they felt a need to reassure Him of their awareness of His great qualities. "You are a truthful man. You teach God's way. Sincerely, you court no favor. You do not act from human respect." This is practically insulting and grossly arrogant. One wonders that Christ did not cut them short as He did others.

They wanted to know how serious He was about an Israel free of foreign domination in according with God's designs. So they put a practical question, "Should we pay taxes to the foreigners.?"

"Show me the tax money."

They had some.

"And whose the head and whose the text?"

He gives them an answer that answers nothing. Everything is God's. They know that. Nothing is the emperor's. They know that, too. But they got the message. He is not interested in political freedom. It is not on His list. He did not come for that. He came for freedom, but of another kind. His rebellion is spiritual. He wages peace.

They were afraid of just that. They left.

This is not late in the Gospels, but early. Later it would be clear. There would be no need to ask. So, Christ knew early what He was about.

In the refectory we have just finished reading the biography of Robert E. Lee. For all his family, his West Point, his military service, he betrayed his country and was guilty of treason. He did it with ease, without great anguish or anxiety. He led the rebellion into our country's most tragic war, Americans killing Americans. He never regretted it, never repented of it, thought it worthy to the end. Gentleman he was, but he was not a man of principle.

Robert McNamara was a major factor in the Vietnam conflict that turned into a monstrous disaster. Later, he too came to see that. Too late though it was, much too late, he came to regret it all and repent of it publicly. There is a principle at work here.

Christ was clear from the outset on goals and the means to them. Violence was out. So was political victory. He preached a gospel of peace, of inner renewal, rebirth, of union with God in grace, of prayer and sacrament, mercy, compassion, the works of justice and peace.

That is the message and this is the work. He laid down His life for it. We are expected to live for it, possibly die for it.

We live in a age of violence. If our age is as violent as any, it is not merely disease and obsession, it is evil, diabolical. The relation of sickness and moral sickness to the Evil One is ancient and scriptural. We are not unaware of the connection.

So whether your world is large or small, claustral or little more, or global in scope, let it be a Christian world founded on principle: Christ and Christ's peace. As Thomas Merton said, "Let God untie the snares of anger and desire in your heart." We preach a gospel all the time. We send out a message. We bear witness of one kind or another. Let it be a message worthy of you, worthy of a Christian.

We repeat with Christ, give Caesar what is his, but to God what is God's. God comes first, and Caesar is God's too.

Blessed are the Poor

MATTHEW 5:1–12

How blessed are you poor.
    The Kingdom of God is yours.
Blessed are you who are hungry now.
    You shall have your fill.
Blessed are you who are weeping now.
    You shall laugh.
    Blessed are you when people hate you,
    drive you out, abuse you,
    denounce your name as criminal on account
    of the Son of Man!
Rejoice when that day comes
    and dance for joy!
    Look; your reward will be great in Heaven.
But alas for you who are rich,
for you are having your consolation.[1]
Alas for you who have plenty to eat now;
    you shall go hungry.
Alas for you who are laughing now,
    you shall mourn and weep.
Alas for you when everyone speaks well of you.
This was the way your ancestors treated the false prophets.[1]

So is it bad when all speak well of you? Is that what He is saying? Is it wrong to be well spoken of? No, you miss the point. That is not what He meant. Being well spoken of is not the idea at all. Living well is. We seek to live well, not to be well spoken of. We do not seek to create an image. We do not cultivate a good public impression, public relations.

[1] The Jerusalem Bible.

First things first. To be well spoken of or poorly, to have a good press or a bad one is irrelevant. What sort of person are you? That's what matters.

So does Christ begrudge us a decent life, enough to eat, a time of laughter?

No, He didn't say that. He asks rather, what is the good life? At what price do you eat well? Who grows your food, who picks it, who packs it, ships it, prepares it, sells it? You eat well. Do they? That is His question.

What are you laughing at? What amuses you? What do you ridicule? What do you make fun of? Whom do you belittle? Who is the butt of your humor? Who pays for it? That is Christ's question. He does not fault your laughter. He only questions the point of it.

In other words, the beatitudes, as we call them, from the first word of the Latin text, *Beati*, are a code of behavior that simply raises questions about your values.

He says it is no sin to be poor. But, to be rich because you are evil and corrupt and crooked is a curse, not a blessing. It will not wear.

Millions go hungry—children most of all—in a country as rich as ours. They are blessed because in comparison with the well-fed and the over-fed, the latter are cursed. Most dogs in our land eat better than some children. No one begrudges a dog a meal, least of all Christ, but something is wrong when dogs eat better than people.

Christ does not love tears and sorrow. He would not have His people a weeping people. But, He says, if you weep as Mine, know this for sure: one day the tears will cease and the weeping vanish, and you will know a joy you cannot imagine.

So, first things first. When you love God and fear Him, and seek to please Him, and live by the law of His love, then things have a way of falling into line. You can keep your balance. You do not lose your good judgment. Then temporary evils are seen for what they are, temporary evils. There are worse things. To be driven out, to be cursed, shunned, denounced, are bad enough, God knows. But, they are not the worst, not when your integrity is intact, your conscience clear. You know in your heart that things will work out. So we rejoice and are glad and dance for joy, no matter what the appearances. We have this from Christ.

Defeating Evil
with the Art of Love

MATTHEW 5:17–37

Salvador Dali has done very strange works of art, weird and wild. He has also done some magnificent religious subjects: the last Supper, the Crucifixion, the Madonna. A special edition of the *Jerusalem Bible* features his studies. His "Temptation of Saint Anthony" is powerful. The passions are depicted as enormous animals with legs three or four stories high. Anger, lust, greed, and pride are depicted as gross exaggerations, unnatural developments that awed Saint Anthony in his prayer. The capital sins are ugly because they are deformed human qualities.

In March, 1947, the police were called to investigate a brownstone mansion on Fifth Avenue, New York, home of the two Collyer brothers. They were bachelors, one a retired lawyer and the other a concert pianist. The lawyer was blind and paralyzed. The other played for him and hoped to cure his blindness by orange juice. He started saving things for his brother to see and read after his cure. The cure never came, but the collecting never ceased. They were found dead in the midst of a house literally packed with stuff. They hauled away one hundred twenty tons of it, including twelve grand pianos and a disassembled Model T Ford. This was as bizarre as any of Dali's animals, and not as rare as one would hope.

Like Saint Anthony, monks know the capital sins, the passions. Indeed, it was the desert monks who first listed and described them in terms familiar to us. We know them in temptations, certainly through a knowledge of the human heart and its potential for evil. Who has not known hints of greed and lust and pride and anger? If we are not Collyer brothers, we know what we could be. Or can we call extravagantly paid stars in the arts, in athletics, and in business, normal, healthy people? Surely there is something sick in the gathering of millions, even billions, superbly expressed by Dali and elegantly displayed by the Collyers.

Our engagement with evil is not fanciful. It is real. In this warfare we join the ranks with St. Benedict under the banner of Christ. We follow a rule and a tradition. We have an abbot, we have one another, we have our customs and practices. We know the grace of God in prayer and sacrament, in holy reading, in work, in the practice of love.

Pious people sometimes think their piety will spare them. Alas, piety may not do if the heart is not as pious as the performance. Christ in the Reading today berates those who belittle the Law. One cannot treat the usages lightly. On the other hand, He insists that what is in the heart is what matters. Mere law abiding will not suffice.

The Irish of an earlier Boston were good Catholic people who loved the Church, were generous and faithful, but they had no use for Negroes, as they called them then. Good, pious Catholics in another century, good pious Catholics from clergy on, had slaves and saw no problem in that. The antagonism of German Catholics to Jews in our era and in the past is not restricted to Germans, their piety notwithstanding. Christopher Columbus was a good and faithful Catholic. He said the Divine Office every day, and his crew sang the *Salve Regina* each night at sea. But when he saw the gentle natives of the Caribbean, his first thought was what beautiful slaves they would make. No one need remind us how staunch Protestants treated American Indians here. Spanish Catholics did the same in South America.

The call then is to constant renewal, unending reformation. The price of liberty is eternal vigilance. Prayer, the grace of God, religion of the heart more than the lips, is the idea. Monastic life is assuredly not just its usages, customs, or rules. Monks, too, can be control freaks, compulsive gatherers, and anxiety-ridden.

The art of love is an arduous business. But it is the only business worth all we put into it. With the help of God's grace we can learn and know Him more clearly, follow Him more nearly, love Him more dearly, day by day.

Good News/Bad News

Mark 9:38–43, 45, 47–48

What do you do with bad news?
What do you do with good news?
I would say the answer probably lies with how you take the priesthood of the Christian people.
During the past two decades nearly half a million Americans have been murdered. An additional 2.5 million have been wounded by gun-fire, more casualties than the U. S. military has suffered in all the wars of the past two hundred years.

The U. S. murder rate today is eight homicides per 100,000 people, about 70% with firearms, 90% by men. The murder rate among men is five times that of Canada, eleven times the rate among men in Germany, twenty times the rate in Ireland or Japan. Among young men aged thirteen to twenty-four in the U.S. the rate has tripled since 1960 and is now about thirty-five times as high as the murder rate among young men in England.

A convicted murderer in the U. S. is released after spending, on average, just six years in prison. At the moment there are about 100,000 convicted murderers locked up in America and perhaps 800,000 living free in American society. Granted the fallibility of figures, it does seem we are a violent society.

A survey by the Center for Media and Public Affairs looked at TV programming in Washington, D.C. on April 7, 1994, and tallied 2,605 acts of violence that day, the majority in early morning when kids were most likely to be watching. By the reckoning of the Cultural Indicators project, the average American child will have witnessed more than 8,000 murders and 100,000 other violent acts on TV by the time he or she leaves elementary school.

Another study, published by the Journal of the American Medical Association in 1992 found that the typical American child spends twenty-seven hours a week watching TV and will witness 40,000 murders and 200,000 other violent acts by the age of eighteen. "Never was a culture so filled with full-color images of violence as ours is now," says one authority.

It would seem that our children are exposed to a great deal of violence. There are social critics who say its effects on society are not evident, that violence on TV does not lead to actual violence. One hopes so. In any case, by any norm, we are violent.

I think a priestly people would respond to this situation.

While infection with AIDS has begun to decline in the western hemisphere, it flourishes in Africa and Asia. Of the 6,000,000 estimated infected worldwide, 2,000,000 are in sub-Sahara Africa, 3,500,000 in Southeast Asia. AIDS flourishes when health conditions are poorest, facilities and finances lacking, and remedies unavailable.

Last year *God's Love: We Deliver*, a volunteer organization, prepared and delivered 540,393 meals free of charge to the house-bound men, women, and children with AIDS in the five boroughs of New York City, and across the river in Hudson County, New Jersey. They also recruited and trained 1,192 new volunteers to work in the kitchen, deliver meals, help with events. The total active number of people was 2,131. In eleven years they have never turned away an eligible client and put no one on a waiting list.

A priestly people would turn to God with thanks for such people, such love.

Tertullian asks, "Are we lay people not priests also? It is written, 'He has made us kings and priests.'"

And Origen, "Do you not recognize that the priesthood has been given to you also, that is to the whole Church of God and the nation of believers? You have therefore a priesthood, being a priestly nation."

And John Chrysostom, "The entire people of God gathered in prayer constitute the fullness of the priesthood."

And St. Augustine, "As we call everyone Christian, so we call everyone priests, because all are members of one priesthood."

The Catechism says, "The whole community of believers is, as such, priestly. The faithful exercise their baptismal priesthood through their participation, each according to his own vocation, in Christ's mission as priest, prophet, and king. Through the sacraments of Baptism and Confirmation the faithful are consecrated to be a holy priesthood."

It would seem, then, that our response to the world scene as much as we know it, would be a priestly one. If the sacramental priesthood makes articulate and explicit the priesthood of all, all follow Christ as priest, prophet, and king. We are priest by the sacrifice of the Cross entered into by our own sacrificial love as vowed by lay people, celibate and married, a single person united to God. We are prophet by the teaching what our life is, the love we are witness to, the sermon we preach by who we are and what we do. We are king by our being responsible for our lives and exercising the dominion we have been given over the world in a manner pleasing to God. As members of communities, local, national, and global, we take our place with a sense of obligation before God.

It is primarily and most effectively in prayer that we are involved in the Christian mystery. Here we are at our noblest as humans. It is our finest hour.

Prayer is adoration and thanks. Prayer is petition and atonement.

At the heart of this cross is Christ. All is in Him, through Him, for Him. We walk with Him, suffer and died with Him and for Him. With Him we love the world and pray for it and with it. Sing him thanks for goodness everywhere and so promote good. Beg for mercy and pardon and healing for all sin and so fight the powers of darkness and evil.

So we all live priestly lives in Christ, the eternal High Priest.

The Dangers of Wealth

MATTHEW 25:14–30

To make *Forbes Magazine's* list of the four hundred wealthiest people in the United States you must have at least $415 million. Toward the bottom of this year's list is one Robert Georgen, for example. He has $490 million. He made it with candles. For $100,000 he and three partners bought a Brooklyn candle factory that sold to churches and religious goods stores. They now do a $331 million business a year, having bought out six competitors along the way. There is money in candles.

To come down in the world a bit, there are 1,300,000 millionaires in our land. That is the latest figure and not updated. There are probably two million now. Twenty years ago there were 120,000. So we do well in millionaires.

The top 20% of households control 47% of our wealth. The average income for the top 20% is $105,000. The bottom 20% average $7,760. We are, of all advanced countries, worst in terms of the gap between rich and poor. It used to be England, but we have long since outdone England. A U.N. report says one in five U. S. children live below the poverty level. We are the worst, 21% below the line. The average low-income child in the seventeen other nations of the industrial West is at least a third better off than a child here. Yet the world's richest children live here.

Talent in the Scriptures means a measure of money. It has come to have the meaning among us as well of any endowment in terms of personal gifts, aptitudes, or native skills. Christ's parable in today's Gospel reading tells us of gifts given and responses made. We are subject to judgment in terms of what use we have made of what God has given us.

Gathering extravagant quantities of money is a use of talent that will never pass a final assessment. That the rich man will hardly enter the Kingdom of Heaven is perhaps a reality. If he does enter, it will not be as a rich man.

We are born to life to know God, to love Him, and to serve Him in this world that we may live with Him forever in the next. Gathering a fortune for yourself is not the service of God. Our talents to serve the common good and give glory to God are meant to be shared.

That said, we can come down to the practical and apply the parable to ourselves. Surely a sense of submission to God's will is in order in terms of what gifts we have or do not have. In terms of what we do have, modest or much, we must develop those gifts for the honor and glory of God. We take what we get and make the best of it. Surely that is the thrust of the parable, a sort of responsible stewardship. We ought to be aware too of our need of gratitude for what we have and invest it for the good of all. Pride is not solved by denying great gifts, but by acknowledging their source. Sin would lie in wasting talent or in using it for ignoble ends. Great gifts of any sort do not make one better. Rather, they exact a developed sense of responsibility.

Forbes Magazine lists our four hundred wealthiest and says of them as a group, "they are super-competitive and always comparing themselves with others. They are obsessively competitive, these highly successful entrepreneurs. Sneer at this competitiveness if you like, but it drives the most productive economy the world has ever seen." Maybe. But it is also the world's sickest economy and most unbalanced. And who ever called Americans *this happy people?*

We have here, we hope, what might be called a mitigated capitalism in our abbey, a Christianized economy. We try to control it. We earn our living. We are satisfied with that. We have a good product and a good price, but we earn to make a living. We do not live to make money. Choir comes before fruitcake. Prayer comes before cheese, not to mention fudge. We need and have quiet and place and a non-aggressive milieu. I do not believe that when Christ taught us to develop talent, He had the *Forbes'* four hundred richest in mind, with an average of over a billion dollars each. This is called greed.

Our efforts to exemplify a good life, well rounded and complete, may hopefully contribute toward building an American way which is more human, more humane, more fair. Surely those of you with families do not nurture greed. Indeed, the struggle to have enough, even a modest amount of prosperity, is endless and at times seems even hopeless.

There will be a reckoning one day over children world wide, but a most severe reckoning here most of all, first of all. Our talents ought to be applied to a worthy end. Our land is not pleasing to God, that is sure.

Internal Evil

LUKE 12:49–53

You would not need a son to appreciate the value of a college with a good sports program as very appropriate to his education. It seems obvious to most. It is not that a son would specifically be a good athlete. Rather, it is the symbolic value of contest that is at point, the dynamism of struggle, of conflict. Surely the main thrust of a great stadium packed with an enthusiastic crowd witnessing a football game is more than what appears. The drawing power of the whole is conflict, contest. Those actually playing—highly trained—the total investment in site, equipment, scheduling, traditional play-offs, act out the hidden drama of elemental involvement with good and evil, mostly unconscious.

The writer of Hebrews draws from the same image. "Since we are surrounded by so great a cloud of witnesses, let us also lay aside every weight and the sin that clings so closely, and let us run with perseverance the race that is set before us."

It is odd to hear Jesus in the Gospel reading today speaking not merely of fire on the earth, but "do you think that I have come to bring peace to the earth? No, I tell you, but rather division! From now on, five in one household will be divided." This does sound off-key for the gentle Jesus who preaches love and mercy, pardon and peace.

But the love and mercy, pardon and peace are against a background of profound commitment to a cause. Ultimately, we are engaged in the conflict of good and evil, in an amalgam of time and eternity, the passing and the permanent, the spiritual and the material. Basically, the warfare is internal, for we meet the enemy there and engage him there. The external is but the reflection of the internal. The basic business and the major work is internal, is spiritual.

Yet the internal is enormously helped by external expression. Love is born in the heart and finds expression in our neighbor. Mercy experienced is revealed in mercy extended to all and any. The outer without the inner in sham, and the inner without the outer will soon wither.

So the dread is that the great conflict acted out in stadium and coliseum nation-wide and world-wide will turn into war-games, and the skills practiced there will be expressed in real war. Then the outer play devoid of inner life turns evil and is expressive of death, not life. The outer war reveals the inner war, where good was defeated and evil triumphed. Out of the heart come greed and lust, hatred and violence.

Hence the fascination with mass conflict, publicly witnessed, whether baseball, basketball, soccer, hockey, or bull-fight. Every witness is a participant in a conflict and knows it, sees it acted out in front of him. If what you learned at Eton, you did at Waterloo, then what you learned was vain. We witness play turned to tragedy, children shooting each other for fun.

We are daily called by Christ to the service of love and the good fight against evil. It is a pity to think "Onward Christian Soldiers Marching As to War" as the ideal Christ had in mind. The war we wage is not with material weapons and against visible enemies. It is, all the same, real war. Count it defeat when you use angry words, ugly temper, anything violent in reference to your neighbor. You are losing the inner battle. Contempt for others, arrogance, fault-finding and judgment reveal the loser.

We are called then to take on the armor of Christ and to practice peace by war against all that is selfish and evil within. The conflict that Christ then predicted would rise between father and son, mother and daughter, is not manifest violence and apparent meanness, but rather an admission that the other asks me to engage in a conflict I cannot abide, want no part of. It is something I cannot stoop to. No contest.

No society is wholly communal nor wholly competitive. The cooperative society will act as one against an enemy and the competitive society can be as communal as any monastery. It is the inner engagement that tells all. Where that is amiss in personal terms or in social ones, nothing will come right and the evil will be expressed externally in injustice, bigotry, violence, abuse, and ultimately war.

The fire Christ came to cast on the earth if the fire of the Spirit burning within, consuming all evil, inspiring every good. Keep that fire brilliant—bright.

A Jarring Note

 **JEREMIAH 20:10–13**
ROMANS 5:12–15
MATTHEW 10:26–33

Life itself is no less a mix than the mix we have in the liturgy these days. If Spring, rather than March, came in like a lamb, and I believe it did, it went out according to pattern, very much like a lion. With impact.

For those who were not around, a mighty wind on the fourth of June at 1:30 P.M. blew off the front roof of the monastery and dumped it in the courtyard, damaged assorted portions of other roofs, not to say laying low hundreds of trees. All within ten minutes and all without injury to us or similarly visited neighbors.

So we now move to the summer solstice, pause, and turn back toward winter and gradually lessening hours of sunshine. In the liturgy the beauty of Corpus Christi—the body and blood of Christ—the Sacred Heart, the Birth of John the Baptist, just came or are about to come. Into the midst of that joyous worship comes Jeremiah the prophet, a jarring note, as a Jeremiad might well be, balanced by Christ's words of comfort and hope to all battered and bruised by life.

We face once again in this day's pondering the ancient mystery of evil, of suffering, and its relation to the good life, the life of the good. One must step carefully in these complex matters and not clumsily plunge ahead, a sure way to make bad matters worse.

Jeremiah predicts trouble of awesome dimensions for his people, and his people, as might be expected, turn on him. "Denounce him! Let us denounce him! We can prevail; we can prevail and take our vengeance on him."

What proves how human that reaction is, is the reaction of Jeremiah. He takes the Lord to task and uses some of the most forceful language of scripture to point out that as a prophet he has been called on, appointed to, a thankless task that has become life-threatening. "You have seduced me, Yahweh, and I have let myself be seduced. You have overpowered me; you were the stronger." Having spoken his mind, Jeremiah feels better, then realizes that he has overdone it, overstated his case. He submits to the Lord.

There is, in the first place, the wisdom to realize that violating the Lord's word will lead to trouble by the very nature of things. God does not intervene to punish. He does not have to. The nature of things itself revolts when violated, and the law of God is written within the nature of things. Much of the evil of this world is such. Most, like Jeremiah, eventually come to see this, and the result is that peoples and societies can come to change their ways and so live more happily.

Much more difficult to deal with is the suffering that comes to the good, or worse, the haphazard quality of so much that comes our own way. We seem mere victims of chance, accident, and circumstance.

To all of this Christ has one answer: fear not, trust in God. Do good and fear not. The human love we have for one another becomes the more human, the more sure, the more faithful, the more it is grounded and rooted in God, in love of God. So, too, our love for life, for the good life, for a life of happiness, joy and peace, becomes more genuine the more grounded in God and the eternal life for which we were born.

When life is all you have, when human love is all you know, disappointment is inevitable. No human love, no earthly happiness, can satisfy the desires of the human heart. We are immortal and immortality is what we must have.

These are the principles that Christ enunciates when He bids us fear only what can kill the soul. Anything less can do us no real harm. If God can be bothered about sparrows, butterflies, daffodils, He can be bothered with us. And is.

No matter what happens, the wild crazy wind notwithstanding, everyone alive seeks Heaven. Christ says He will take care that we get there. And so we hope.

It is good to enunciate these truths, make them articulate, for they have great power. They nourish the soul, deepen and enrich life, are a firm foundation in a shaky world. This is life real, to live in reality, in the truth. Any life that does not ponder these truths is not merely shallow, but it is basically unreal, fanciful. But with them we can manage good days and bad, hard times and soft, wild winds and lovely feasts.

Living with Compassion and Mercy

MARK 10:2–16

One feels a certain amount of compassion for a parish priest who must face a congregation today of young and old, single, married, widowed, divorced, divorced and remarried, with a gospel incident that lays out Christ's teaching on divorce in the boldest, clearest terms: it is forbidden.

In the face of a culture that takes a benign attitude toward it, Catholics are as benign as any others. Yet, even in an age of more frequent divorce, the original vows are usually taken with a pledge of permanent love till death. Though some are not marriages at all and are declared such for some defect, most *are* marriages. So the divorced are placed in a position that can be questioned. This is an addition to the sadness of a dream gone and a lovely promise come to naught. When there are children, there is genuine tragedy. Divorce looks easy. It isn't. It is very hard on everyone. So any sort of judgment by a monk, for example, seems uncalled for. Prayer, compassion, and hope, do seem called for.

We witness the enormous impact of our peers. We are likely to see ourselves immune—as monks—and yet, as monks we do every bit as poorly as those around us. Notwithstanding careful screening, years of preparation, highest motivation, good example, for this reason and for that—it's always plausible—they depart by way of being dispensed of what they solemnly promised. Granted, we are not dealing with a sacrament. Granted there are no children involved. Granted it is all licit and provided for by law, it is still the end of a dream, a promise come to naught. We do seem called to more than a plausible life.

We witness here, therefore, the poverty of the human scene, our frailty, and how powerfully moved by the world we live in, even we who live, as it were, separated from that world. Yet this world is more a world of spirit than a secular society, for there are trends and fashions and enthusiasms that move through the human psyche world-wide, sweep through the human spirit in some mysterious way. What goes on here, goes on everywhere. What goes on everywhere, goes on here.

I hope there will be no offense in my calling to mind personal history and my years with the Divine Word missionaries. They came to the United States one hundred years ago (1884) this October. They were not long on the scene as missionaries, as foreigners, before they were appalled at the condition of black people. There were no priests among them. Worse than that, no black was received in a Catholic school, in a Catholic college or university, in a seminary. These foreigners found this situation shameful. They did something about it. Since no one else would, they opened a seminary for blacks, and by 1934 had four ordained, splendidly trained. One of the first four was Father Vincent Smith from nearby Lebanon. He later, in 1948, joined the monks here. The legend was that his heart was broken. White bishops, white priests, white people, did not welcome a black priest. Dom James included him as Father Simon in the first group sent to the new foundation in New York, near Rochester, now Genesee Abbey. He died there.

The dream goes on. Christ dreamed of a Church, His Body, His Bride, one with Him, one with one another. Look at it, split into countless fragments, dismembered, and disorganized. What a pity. What a shame. And what a revelation.

In the face of which we watch our answer. We do not judge, we do not point fingers, we do not accuse. We have compassion and we have mercy. People do what they can with what they have. Granted that they blunder and falter. They often reveal human poverty and frailty more than anything else.

In the face of which we turn to Christ. If anyone is to condemn, let Him do it. For our part, we do what we can to break down walls, build love, span chasms of separation, and work to unite man to woman, parent to child, all the flock to one Shepherd, all humankind to another.

Despite all the mess, we do not lose hope. Nor do we take the easy route and point, find fault, condemn. We point the finger within our own fickle heart. There we thank God we are hopefully still with Him, and ask Him to keep us so, and speak without end for all our brothers and sisters.

Notwithstanding all appearances, we are one. Christ makes it so.

Loving One on One

MATTHEW 11:28-30

When Brother Maurice, now Father Maurice, Brother Meinrad and I, some twenty-five years ago were in Oxford, North Carolina, in a small experimental community, a friend of the place, Jim Connell, brought us a bevy of young Guinea hens as a gift, about fifteen of them. The gift was welcome. Guinea hens are attractive, great watchdogs, and lovers of community, for they are constantly together. This protects them, for they fly hardly at all. Our friend told us, "These are from two settings, though they were together after only a day or two from hatching. They will probably know that." And so it was. They split into two groups, each having nothing to do with the other. The others were foreigners.

Going back further, in two years of college before the major seminary, some hundred of us were gathered from three minor seminaries, one in the Boston area, one in the Chicago area, and one in Dubuque, Iowa. Those from the east were mostly Irish, those from the midwest were mostly Polish, and those from the west were mostly German. We did a great deal of hiking on free days. The groups had to have three or four people; you submitted a list. There had to be one from each area, at least. So, we were forced to know one another, understand and appreciate one another, however different. We would likely not have done it without coercion. It was simply part of the course for a missionary order.

Though we are a nation born of a mix of people, we do nonetheless keep alive a lot of prejudice in race, color, nationality, and religion. The recent outbreak of arson involving black churches looks suspiciously racist. It is no secret that racism is very much alive in some areas.

Sometimes we betray our true feelings in a chance remark. It does no good to hide your prejudice. It will eventually come out and perhaps do great harm, very great. It is like the youngster who lit a packet of firecrackers to scare people in a fireworks shop. It set the store afire and eight people died in the stampede out the door. All this from a small prank, and by one mentally retarded it turns out. Prejudiced people are spiritually retarded, and by their own choice.

You no doubt read of supreme court justice Clarence Thomas returning to the Faith after an estrangement of twenty-eight years. He early on wanted to be a priest, and entered Immaculate Conception Seminary in Missouri after high school seminary. That he was black made a difference and he was aware of it. Under the assault his Faith began to erode. On the day Martin Luther King, Jr., was shot in 1968, he overheard a seminarian say, "I hope the SOB dies." "It was the straw that broke my back," Thomas said. The remark was costly, very costly. It was a firecracker in a fireworks shop.

I am not aware of prejudice in the abbey, though there may be some. Or, it may be hidden. In any case, it is a flawed Christianity that looks askance on any person. We are not misogynists, or anti-Semites, or anti-Hispanics, or anti-any other humans. If we are, it must be purged from our hearts by the grace of God. The trouble is, of course, that we can be prejudiced and not realize it, for we have always been so. It would seem to me that a life of prayer and quiet and community would soon reveal a hateful heart, in submission to the yoke that is easy and a burden that is light.

Like Guinea hens, we do prefer our own kind. We are most comfortable with them.

One of our monasteries admitted a number of gay men. Gays make as good monks as any when properly qualified. But the young men stuck too close together. It was reverse prejudice. So they had to let them go for lacking a sense of community, indeed Christian, Catholic love.

It is not an even picture, past or present. Some things are worse, many better. Certainly in the Church things are better. It is now acknowledged that interracial marriages are very much on the rise. Granted, we are a society of heightened racial polarization, intensified group solidarity, and increased hostility between groups. However, more and more blacks and whites are doing a curious thing: falling in love with each other, notwithstanding whatever is happening in the public policy area. When it is one to one, there seems to be less racism. Since 1967, it is no longer forbidden in nineteen states to marry interracially.

Surely one on one is the best answer. Love in general is not impressive. Individual love is. We believe in love and try to live in love for the simple reason that it is Christian. Hopefully, by grace and example, we spread love in a world that can use it. Love may be "a harsh and dreadful thing," as Dostoyevski put it, but not only. Not wholly. Not really. The cross may be the center of our Faith, but the resurrection is its sequel. The yoke is easy, and the burden is light, because He said so.

Purple Curtain

In fourth year English in the minor seminary we were doing he poetry of Edgar Allan Poe. Joe Coughlin, who was from Brooklyn, was reading aloud the poem *The Raven*. When he came to the famous lines, he did them in Brooklynese: "And the silken, sad, *unsoitin* rustling of the *poiple coitan*s thrilled me"—the class broke into laughter and Fr. Kraus said, "That will be enough of you, Mr. Coughlin."

We used to have a Lenten *poiple coitan* floor to ceiling that marked off the sanctuary for that season. It was not a total block-out, but was rather thin material. It was opened for the consecration in the Mass.

The tradition is still around in the veiling of crucifixes and statues in purple during Lent. A last vestige remains in the veiled cross of Good Friday. And even that is optional.

The idea was, of course, sin. Sin darkens vision, the vision of God, of faith. It erects a barrier between us and Heaven: God and the angels and the saints. Penitence helps remove that.

Besides, it is to cultivate reverence and awe for holy things. The cult of the secret. Eastern churches often use an icon screen back of which the liturgical action takes place. In great cathedrals of the past, the high altar was not necessarily visible to all. The choir stalls in front of it, sometimes a rood screen or other piece blocked the view. Lesson and Gospel were chanted and could be heard. The canon was silent. A bell rung at offertory, sanctus, consecration, and communion made known where the action was at any moment.

Matters are quite otherwise today. All is open visible, vocal, and intelligible. And like Jesus on the cross, the priest faces us and prays in our tongue.

Perhaps we need no purple curtain to remind us that sin interrupts converse with God. The world around us is a message clear enough. Nor must we once again make a litany of the woes of our dreadful time. We see sin and the fruits of it. And since we came from that same world and carry it with us in our hearts, we cope with all against evil and live love.

I wrote the *Courier Journal* yesterday, not a letter for publication, but with a suggestion: that they reprint a page they did a couple of years ago: photos and brief data on Kentucky's thirty-nine prisoners on Death Row in Eddyville. I suggested they print it on Good Friday. Without any comment.

I don't think comment is called for. Putting people to death for a punishment or as a lesson to society is a travesty of justice and an outrage too gross to stomach. That mistakes are made proves it.

President Bush in his years as Texas governor signed death warrants for 122, and is proud of it. Even in the case of a paranoid schizophrenic, with personal pleas from John Paul II and the signed petition for mercy from heads of state in Europe, he went ahead.

This is a nation with one of the highest murder rates in the world, of the highest prison population, it is a nation of violence and ugly greed, starving children and hordes of homeless. Who needs a Lenten curtain?

So Christ continues to be put to death in His people. The Passion goes on. "What you do to the least, you do to Me." I presume this is not poetic fancy.

> "For in the wreckage of your April Christ lies slain,
>   and Christ weeps in the ruins of my spring."[1]

And we know that the Mass is not a mere ceremonial recall of a two-thousand year old event, but a living sacrifice of death in every sense of the word. Christ continues to be put to death and He makes of that death a cry of mercy to His Father and of forgiveness to those who so sinned.

The last Mass will be offered when the last crime is committed. When no hand is raised against brothers, no violence done in thought or word or deed. No love betrayed. Then will the End come.

Our response to all this is not condemnation, accusation. We each

---

[1]   Thomas Merton, "For My Brother: Reported Missing in Action, 1943," *Collected Poems of Thomas Merton* (New Directions Press, 1948).

have a heart and the human heart is a mysterious amalgam of good and evil which only God and grace can heal.

And that is the business we are about: to heal the human heart, starting with this one: our own.

There is no greater, more noble, more necessary work. And every Christian is called to it. If there is a poet, and artist, a dancer, a singer, a dreamer, a mystic in everyone—and there must be, otherwise poets and priests and mystics and artists would starve—then our response in grace as monks is merely making articulate what everyone who is Christ's is engaged in; indeed, everyone who is God's, since so many others share these concerns.

Purple is blue with a lot of red. Today (*Laetare* Sunday), traditionally, priests can wear rose vestments. Rose is purple carried far into red, more blood in a sense, more warmth, more love. And that should characterize the heart that looks out on this world with Jesus on the cross: He who said, "If I be lifted up, I will draw all to Myself"—in mercy and pardon, obviously, in grace and peace. Amen.

6 ~ Sacraments

Touching Fire

John 20:19–31

There are two kinds of travelers to the Holy Land, especially to Jerusalem: tourists and pilgrims. A tourist moves from the center of his existence, his home, to the periphery. He is on vacation. A pilgrim moves from the periphery, to the center of the world, his home.

It has been noted in the Jerusalem medical world that there is a tendency to breakdown among pilgrims. One doctor has treated hundreds in the last ten years. Most of them had previous problems, but many not. Overwhelmed by profound spiritual experience, they come suddenly to fancy themselves Jesus, Mary, the Messiah, or one of the prophets. The treatment is not difficult; it is effective. Usually it is all over in a week and becomes total and final when they leave. They return to normal and wonder whatever happened to them. People in the Israel tourist trade are familiar with all this, called popularly the "Jerusalem Syndrome," and know all the tell-tale signs. The first is to fall behind your tour group. Then irritation with them all. Then comes preaching. Finally, one goes around in a bed sheet. Members of the Israeli Army, should they find a European or American wandering in white looking for locusts and honey, simply take the person to the psychiatric hospital in northwest Jerusalem. The head doctor there says it is not true psychosis, but a religious casualty. People get too close to fire and catch on fire themselves.

A kindergarten teacher believed for a week that she was pregnant with the new messiah, then returned to Maine and to her husband and job and didn't say a word about it. A pastor from the midwest went on a tour of the Holy Land with his wife. As he stood before Golgatha he acquired a fierce belief that he was Jesus returned to earth. After five days he returned to the midwest, to his pulpit. Among the listening parishioners only his wife knew about his brief fling with divinity. A computer programmer from New York City visited Jerusalem in 1994 and was suddenly seized by the worry that he might be Jesus. If so, what should he do?

One comment suggests that likely candidates for the syndrome are Catholics and the Orthodox who love ritual, rite, ceremony, and liturgy. Not so. Ninety-five percent of the cases are Protestant.

The doctor says that for Protestants the religious hierarchy has been broken. They have direct access to God and that enables one to have a strong personal experience. But the loss of ritual, the loss of the sacramental tradition, is dangerous under stressful conditions. Ritual is a psychic machinery by which the believer can get close to God, to the fire, without getting burnt.

Ruth Barnhouse, a psychiatrist and Episcopal priest, agrees. The Protestant stands alone before God. This is the strength and weakness of Protestantism. Obviously, it is an advantage to stand face to face with God. But it can have serious psychological consequences.

We can rejoice in the healthiness of our Faith. In today's Gospel reading, Christ speaks of the forgiveness of sins, and He passes the power to the Apostles that they forgive in his Name.

The entire ritual of going to confession, telling your sins, receiving absolution from God, from Christ, by way of the priest is good for us in so many ways. Not only are our sins forgiven, Christ's grace restored or increased, the love of God once again made a quality of our life—but it is all done in a human, humane way.

God forgives our sins the moment we repent of them, but there is healing for us in hearing it.

One can worship God in the woods, on the mountains, in the privacy of one's room—but it is so healthy also to do so with others—to kneel, to pray, to sing, to receive peace and give it, to hear the Word, to eat the Bread of Life, to drink the Cup of Salvation. All very human and humane.

Our life in the Church, our response to it is so sound, so healthy, but we are used to it and may forget that, or not realize it. And the fruit of it is not some bizarre experience, but a deep peace, a sense of meaning, and in the midst of whatever comes, a kind of joy that is deeper than mere feeling, mere mood. We are grateful to God.

The Drama of Reality

 LUKE 9:11–17

The Eucharist is "the source and summit of the Christian life. It is the efficacious sign and sublime cause of that communion in the divine life and that unity of the people of God by which the Church is kept in being. It is the culmination both of God's action sanctifying the world in Christ and the worship we give to Christ and through Him to the Father in the Holy Spirit. By the Eucharistic celebration we already unite ourselves with the heavenly liturgy and anticipate eternal life when God will be all in all." So the Documents say.

Merely to list the titles by which we identify the Eucharist indicates its inexhaustible riches. We call it:

> Eucharist – Thanksgiving
> The Eucharistic Assembly
> The Memorial of the Lord's Passion and Rising
> The Holy Sacrifice
> The Holy and Divine Liturgy
> The Sacred Mysteries
> The Most Blessed Sacrament
> Holy Communion
> Holy Mass

Corpus Christi is a classic expression of medieval piety with Mass, procession, and exposition of the Sacrament, giving a particular emphasis to the Eucharist as presence, besides food and sacrifice. In contemplating the mystery in a different context and different rites, we deepen our grasp in faith of what is ineffable.

Similarly, one might think of the sacrament in terms of drama, of play. Play is an age-old effort to express reality in terms that deepen our understanding. Drama is life as viewed by a bystander. One pulls back from the real in order to understand it better.

We can see sanctuary as stage, priest as actor, people as witnesses, as participants. No participants, no drama. We deal with setting, costume, lighting, ritual. The priest says, in effect, "Let us play. I will be Christ. I will take bread on a plate. I will take wine in a cup. I will say over the bread, not this is His Body, for I act in the role of Christ, but this is My Body. I will say over the cup, not this is His Blood, but this is My Blood given for you. We offer them to the Father—the separated Body and Blood expressing His death since body and blood were separated in Him.

This Christ is offered to the Father in atonement for sin, and the sin is forgiven in the mercy of God. He embraces us in love, bids us come forward and eat and drink with Him at the holy table.

Having done so, we are dismissed and sent back into the world. "Having put Me to death, let be. Abandon evil for good now, hate for love, condemnation for mercy."

Our faith tells us that we put Him to death by our sins. In the Eucharist we confront again what we have done, beg pardon, receive forgiveness, and are graced with His love and life. The Mass is profoundly traumatic.

The play, the drama, the theater of it is all reality. Here make-believe, pretending, acting, cross the threshold of what is real and become living history.

Yet the Mass is not Calvary repeated. It cannot be repeated. It *is* Calvary, Calvary carried on through time until the end. Here we enter into stage time, dream time, mythic time, mystic time, God's time—the ultimately real. Hence, our engagement is real, our involvement as real as our sins, which are real indeed.

"Where you there when they crucified my Lord?" Yes. This morning.

It is no wonder that some of His disciples withdrew when He first started talking about this mystery. They were the first to withdraw. There have been many since.

Even Catholics who avoid Mass reveal meaning by doing so. It can be more than mere indifference. It can be, rather, some canny instinct that is aware of the true meaning of it all. Like an animal sensing danger—a fragile bridge, thin ice—which is simply too challenging.

The Mass is everything. You cannot get used to it anymore than you can get used to another new day, another week, another year. Each is unique, a fresh creation. The Mass is one and whole and simple. Yet, in God's Now we have it with us new every new day. Drama indeed, until the final curtain.

The Fruit of Evil

LUKE 4:1–13

Many years ago, so many, in fact that it seems in a previous incarnation, I was called home from a mission assignment in the Pacific to do some other work. I returned by way of Europe—as close that way as the other—and so got a look at a few other countries. I do not remember much, but I do remember this—Europe was clean, some lands immaculate.

I thought of that last week when I went to see two doctors, one in Lebanon and one in Campbellsville, named fittingly for a monk's care, Kirk and Angel. The roads over one way and back another were unsightly with litter, lots of litter, scattered along the wayside. Why do Americans do this? They did not bring it with them from Europe and most of them are from Europe ultimately. Why do they do it here? Foreign visitors are appalled. It is an ugly trait, unsightly, selfish, arrogant, thoughtless. Despite years of effort to eradicate this vice, small progress has been made. Why do they dump their trash in my front yard? They don't do it at home.

Americans have many good qualities, but this is not one of them. It is disgraceful. People otherwise decent open the window, throw out the debris, and move on down the road.

So I was thinking about this. What is going on here? I suggest it is rooted in guilt.

Americans are a favored people. They live in one of the richest, best developed, most beautiful countries in the world. Who would argue with that? Further, they are daily exposed to how the rest of the world lives, and that in vivid and dramatic terms. It is absurd to suggest that has no impact. Famine, disease, poverty, ignorance, tyranny, oppression are common. The lot of most.

And we live in Paradise. Why? What is so special about us? Nothing really. Just happenstance. Providence, fortune, good luck.

A person can feel guilty about it in some unconscious way. We know, in our hearts, that we are not as deserving as we would like to think So we act out our guilt. We do something nasty. Everyone knows that throwing your trash on the roadside is nasty. Maybe this makes you feel better, thinking, "I'm not special. I'm just a sinner and a slob in paradise."

But guilt is not resolved by acting out evil. When a child gives in to impulse and, instead of being its usual self, does something mean, we correct the child. That's not how you deal with an evil impulse. You confess it. You acknowledge it. You ask mercy and forgiveness. But you do not act on it. Otherwise, we simply confirm ourselves in evil.

Granted that litter is not a major moral problem; it is a highly significant one, one worth considering.

If confession is extraordinarily healthy for moral growth, the Eucharist is even more so. In the Eucharist we are confronted with the fruit of evil.

The Mass is no mere re-enactment of the Passion and Death of the Lord. Ritual re-enactment it is, but it is also reality. It *is* the death of the Lord.

That is why the head is a priest, and why he stands at an altar. He is offering a sacrifice as Christ. This Christ is put to death, by sinners, and we are sinners. So in the truest sense we witness the consequences of our evil. Our evil put the Son of God to death.

His death becomes a merciful pardon and healing. We are forgiven by the Lord we crucified and invited to His table to be united to Him in His Body and Blood, Soul and Divinity.

Then we are bidden to go home and live in love. There is now no need to act out evil in us. We have already done so. In His merciful grace we can live in love.

Here is the healing of guilt. We are sinners healed by the mercy of God. Now there is no need to come to terms with guilt by acting on it. We both resist evil and receive pardon. Guilt is overwhelmed by the mercy of God.

In many ways, large and small, serious and trifling, we may reveal a guilt-ridden heart. Acting out is not the answer. Pardon is the answer, pardon through confession and God's mercy, pardon through the passion in which the very death we inflicted on the Lord becomes our salvation.

These are deep truths. They are worth reflecting on these days.

Can You Forgive?

Some twenty years ago a World War II story emerged, the memory of a man who heard a confession he could not absolve.

A young Jew is taken from a death camp to a nearby makeshift army hospital. He is led to the bedside of a Nazi soldier whose head is completely bandaged. The dying Nazi blindly extends his hand toward the Jew and in a cracked whisper begins to begins to speak. The Jew listens silently while the Nazi confesses to having participated in the burning alive of an entire village of Jews. The soldier is terrified of dying with this burden of guilt, and begs absolution from the Jew.

Having listened to the Nazi's story for several hours, torn between horror and compassion for the dying man, the Jew finally walked out of the room without speaking.

Was his action right? Or wrong?

That is the point of Simon Wiesenthal's book, *The Sunflower* (Schochen Books, New York). The second half consists of a couple of dozen answers from eminent people: writers, scientists, theologians, professional people, etc. Of course, the reader is having the same question put to him or her.

Can you forgive someone who has done evil to others? I think the Christian answer would be, "No, only God can forgive sins."

We can forgive injury and evil done to ourselves, but that is really a personal participation in the mercy and forgiveness of God. Ultimately, only God can forgive sin. As Christians we are bidden to forgive injury done to us, both to express our position as sinners in need of mercy and as Christians who know that in the end it is the mercy of God that matters.

A Jew may be unable to forgive the Nazis for what they did to Jews, and in a sense is in no position to do so. But he can surely pray for mercy for them all, as they come before the judgment of God, knowing that he too in however modest or major a way is a sinner also in need of mercy.

Perhaps what the Jew in the story should have done was to try and find a priest, perhaps not too difficult in a Nazi death camp. The dying man was twenty-one years old and a Catholic who had repudiated his faith when he joined the Hitler Youth and later the sadistic and savage SS division of Hitler's armed forces.

Or, he could have told the young soldier, "To forgive you is more than I can do, but I can surely pray that God will do so and I will join you in prayer for that." The young Nazi was not content with throwing himself onto the mercy of God, but wanted, in the style of his Catholic youth, to tell his sins to someone as he once told them to Christ in the person of the priest. So now he confesses them to a Jew as representative of all Jews, and especially of the ones he killed.

We ought sometime to recall how blessed we are in the Sacrament of Reconciliation, the forgiveness of sins, confession. The burden of guilt that sin brings is devastating and lifelong. It is all very well to know that God forgives when we turn to Him for mercy, but for the human it is a fragile business. We have no assurance that He has done so, no word of pardon. On the other hand, to come clean with our sin, to accept responsibility for it, to go to the trouble of going to confession, to do some self-examination of conscience, and most of all, to tell our pathetic story to another human, may add up to an ordeal. But if it is an ordeal, it is rich with the blessings of peace and grace. It is faith at work. We tell our sins to Christ and it is Christ who forgives. No mere man can do that. The words of absolution are the words of Christ. A great burden is removed from the heart and we are grateful to God.

It is surely not good for your health in any sense, spiritual, mental, physical, or emotional, to carry a burden of guilt. Even common sense will tell you, confess your sins and get right with God. There is much happiness in it. We are sinners all, but when we acknowledge as much, then we are forgiven sinners, and that is something else again.

There is a kind of social dimension to confession, not only in the sense that through it we are restored to full communion with God, His grace, the Church, the community—and we are—but as penitents we express sorrow for sin to God. All sin, all evil. It is a contribution to the cause of good, a stand against the dark forces of evil, a statement for good. We may not be responsible for the evil done around us in the world, but we do take responsibility for our own evil and so contribute to the cause of God and His kingdom.

Have a merciful heart and so win mercy. "Forgive us our trespasses as we forgive those who trespass against us."

7 ~ Death

A Homily for the Passing of Patsy Ann

 When we stand before the Mystery of death we are at a complete loss. It is beyond us. It is mystery in the classic sense—a truth which surpasses human understanding. It is as mysterious as life itself. In fact, birth is a kind of analogy of death. The child in the womb is blissfully happy, content to be where it is. But one day it necessarily must leave the womb for a life it knows nothing about, in no way can conceive of or understand.

The passage to that new life can be very painful. So can our death. We have no particular desire to leave a world we know and love, the only world we know. Yet leave we must, often painfully, to enter into a new life far surpassing any human understanding—eternal glory in the bliss of God's presence.

We have that in faith. It is not fantasy, make-believe, a mere wish. It is a matter of faith made possible in Christ. He, too, was born. He lived, suffered, died, and rose from the dead. That whole history reveals in full the purpose of life and its possibility. In that faith we take our stand. However sad, death is birth to life, a passage to glory through the passion, death and rising of Christ.

Death, then, is a call to faith, faith in a most stressful situation, in the depth of sorrow. The grace of that faith freely given by God makes it possible to pass through tears to joy that one we love is born to eternal happiness. We join her in her passing with our prayer that she be born already now into life with God forever. To witness death and believe in life is to respond in depth to the very purpose of one's existence—is the key to assuaging our grief and strengthening our faith. May she rest in peace.

What did They do?

During the forty days after the rising of Christ from the dead, it is not particularly difficult to imagine what the disciples did. They surely gathered in groups large and small and talked together about what had happened since the Lord entered their lives. There is healing in sharing, and in this sharing something new was created. The Gospel story began to take shape and the genesis of the Church, that creative gestation before the coming of the Spirit and the birth of the Church on earth.

Overwhelmed, bewildered, and frightened, Christ's own went back over the last three years—maybe it wasn't even three—and tried in some way to put it all together, if only by remembering what He said, what He did, and where, and when. The historical myth began to develop, oral history in formation. Now and again perhaps—who knows how many times and in what circumstances—Christ Himself took His place among them for comfort and encouragement, filling in details perhaps, or being sure their memory was correct. Distraught they surely were, overcome by reality. In a state of shock, no doubt.

Primitive people I knew when I lived in New Guinea found our rites of death and watch, of burial and mourning, unbelievably brief. It is all over in a few days, and then back to work. Life goes on. We do mourn, of course, and often a long time, but it is a private grief. Theirs was public and prolonged.

If that seems a human reaction to the mystery of death and loss, what state would the apostles, the disciples, have been in, given Who He was and what He did? The enormity of His tragic death, following so soon after by His glorious return to life. It's a bit much to cope with.

Do you suppose they broke the bread and drank the cup in His memory, even before He was wholly gone in the flesh? Who knows?

What we do know is that they gathered and talked and prayed, and waited. What next?

We can see at this distance the marvel that was shaping their days. Call it the beginning of the liturgical life, to use professional terms. We, too, gather as they did, we reminisce, as they did. We tell again the familiar story, as they did, and then act it out in the memorial meal, as they did.

Yet, it was far more than mere memory. We know what they cannot have grasped yet, that Christ lives on in His mysteries, and in the events of His life. It is not just memory, not even when the story took particular shape and was put down in writing. We do not merely read the story or hear it read, we do it.

We do it time and time again for a lifetime. The whole cycle of the year is the story told from beginning to end, and the story is re-enacted, entered into, and lived. In that sense, we mourn the death of Jesus for a lifetime, and we celebrate His birth and all else to the Rising, over and over, each time hopefully in grace and gift, grasp just a bit more of what it all means.

The gift of a long life means a repeated participation in the greatest of human events. In terms of salvation, once is enough. In terms of full grasp, a lifetime is but a beginning. One Christmas, one Holy Week, one Easter, one Pentecost, would do. Yet who could say even a lifetime of the mystical life is enough? Rather, only eternity will suffice.

So, by some strange Providence we have been caught up in some magnificent drama of enormous consequence for the world, for time, and for eternity. It has happened as casually and as innocently as the call of the first ones. He came walking down the shore of the lake one day and said, now to this one, now to that one, "Come, follow me." They could in no way have sensed what it would mean. Neither can we. We have some smidgen of understanding of what we are about in His grace, but not much more.

So we gather in prayer, we talk about Him, we hear the story again, and we break the bread and drink the cup and are seized up in the mystery of God come among us. The salvation of the world is in it all.

How blessed are we.

A Great Day

LUKE 3:10–18

"From a sudden and unprovided death, deliver us, Lord."
This petition is from the Litany of the Saints, heard at ordination vows and at the Holy Saturday baptismal rite. The needs are always there, if the petitions are not. Sudden death is never welcome, and to die unprepared seems tragic to the pious. So, one prays for a seasonable death and time for repentance. "Pray for us sinners now at the Hour of our death."

Father Louis' (Thomas Merton) death was sudden. One thinks of it also as provident and provided. His whole Asian journey was a pilgrimage, so his state of soul would have been appropriate to any design of God. His death was in the design of God, the point of pilgrimage, which is what Jean Leclercq had in mind, presumably, when told the news in Bangkok, "C'est magnifique!" "How splendid a leave-taking," as if Father Louis had staged it.

It was Tuesday in the second week of Advent at Gethsemani, meaning Gethsemani Farms work for most, and that for some weeks. Father Timothy was the reader at the noon meal. The book was a biography of Pierre Teilhard de Chardin. As the meal came to a close, Abbot Flavian got up from his place, walked to the reader's table, signed the reader to stop, picked up the microphone and said, "Brothers, I have sad news for you. Father Louis has died in Bangkok. That's all I know. I'll let you know as soon as I hear more." We said the closing meal prayer and the day went on.

The abbot had received the message at 10:00 that morning. The telegram read, "Abbot Burns. Trappist P.O. Gethsemani, KY. Department regrets to inform you the following message received for you from

184

American Embassy Bangkok Thailand. 'Informed by Abbot Weakland that Thomas Merton has died.' Mr. Hobart Luppi, Director Speical Consular Services. Department of State."

Father Louis had died on Wednesday the 11th at around 3:00 or earlier in the afternoon. It was Tuesday the 10th here, twelve hours behind. We were getting up for Vigils.

* * *

Some years ago I traveled by horse with a Father along mountain tracks for some six hours or more in cold, heavy rain. The trail was dangerous, slippery shale, soft mud, steep drops. We often had to lead the horses. When the little mission center finally came into view, Father Gehlen said to me, "Someone's on the front porch waiting out the rain. I know who it is. It's the Seventh Dav Adventist pastor. I don't care, though. After all this cold and wet, we're going to have a glass of rum, despite his views on Rome and rum." Which we did.

After a change, we sat down for a small visit. In the midst of the small talk, he said, "It's gonna be a Great Day." I said, "Sir?" He said, "It's gonna be a Great Day."

"What do you mean?"

"You know. Armageddon, the Valley of Jehosephat, and the Final Judgment."

I was so taken aback I laughed. He was puzzled that I laughed. I told him that Catholics believe in the Second Coming as much as he did and were doing it long before there were any Seventh Day Adventists. "He will come again in glory to judge the living and the dead, and His Kingdom will have no end." It's in the Mass. "We wait in joyful hope for the coming of our Savior." "But," I said, "we hardly have it up front all the time. It's rather an unconscious awareness, but an awareness for all that. We think about death, too, but don't have a casket ready in the basement."

Death is our first encounter with the Last Day. Advent is a preparation for such, both our own and the ultimate. We are deeply involved in both. We shall all die in turn, and we will all be present at the Last Great Day. However, late, however early, and assuredly sudden, whenever.

It would seem we pray that the end—either of them—be not too sudden. Most of all not "improvisa morte" not a death unprovided for.

The first is an appropriate petition, the last, essential. We trust the Lord understands that.

Today is Gaudete Sunday, "Rejoice" Sunday. You can wear colorful vesture exceptionally if you like. Yet, ours is not a joyful age. Most who know us do not see Americans an especially happy people. We don't look it. Not to others. Maybe not even to ourselves.

The Southwest Indians said to Carl Jung about white people, "Why are they so angry?" How we look is not the major interest, of course.

But there is no need to be glum because the end is coming, yours, mine, all creation. It may be sudden. I'd say your happiness is a good sign that you're provided for. I mean to say, you are right with God, with me, with all your brothers and sisters, yourself and everyone else. That being so, be glad you have work, can pray, are adequately housed and fed, clothed and cared for, warm and dry in a setting of beauty and peace. You have reason, may it be said, to rejoice. So have I. If by some gift I could tell you how much longer you've got, perhaps your joy would only increase. Even so, this is someone's last Advent.

It was a significant trip for Father Louis. And his last. It's gonna be a Great Day, as the man said. Sudden if it be, if it must. Provided for, certainly. Hopefully, not too soon. There's no hurry.

What's Your Color

LUKE 12:35–40

All Souls Day is the only feast day when the celebrant, as far as I know, has a choice of colors for his vesture. He can wear black or purple or white.

Black, of course, was for long centuries the color that went with death. I do not think so much as mourning or somber, sullen or resented grief, as rather seriousness. Death is a serious matter. Let it be treated seriously, in dignity and restraint. After all, black is still the appropriate dress at a very formal affair, certainly for the male and sometimes his partner. If the bride is in white, the groom is often in black. Not somber, but serious.

Since a fairly recent custom permits a priest three Masses today, I wore purple for two out of three. Offering three Masses nowadays is no more a privilege but a necessity for many an overburdened priest. But, I did not wear black. We sent our black vestments to the poor of Russia.

But I did wear purple. Surely the best of colors, warmer than blue and not so radical as red, but something of each, a color of honor and dignity. It is for bishops and monsignors and is the penitential color of Advent and Lent. The elegance of purple, royal purple, will call to mind in Advent the ultimate coming as well as the proximate, the final one. The purple of Lent moves us to penitence with Christ on His way to the Cross, for purple is close to heavenly blue and the red of blood and suffering.

White is now in favor as symbolic of the joy of Heaven. There is the joyous aspect to death as birth to the eternal life won for us in Christ. We temper grief with hope and soften sorrow with an awareness of the glory that follows our end on earth.

A lifetime ago black was favored by clerics, but not, I think, as

187

somber and sad. The black clothes set them apart somewhat as men engaged in serious matters: birth and life and death, sacrament and sacrifice and anointing, teaching and baptizing and marrying and burying. All serious engagement with human life, and their dress showed it.

They liked black cars too, Cadillacs for bishops. Indeed, in those early tight days only bishops and gangsters could afford them. Not that Catholics begrudged them. They had precious little themselves, but they had beautiful churches and were proud that their bishop lived in a fine house, had a grand car. If they were nobodies, he wasn't.

We are no longer into black or Cadillacs, or gangsters being shot on the front steps of the church, the priest photographed kneeling over the prostrate figure anointing him. Days later another front page feature with the splendid funeral at the Italian parish, together with three cars of flowers. Our neighbors were shocked at this mixture of crime and piety, the zany mix of ugly and holy, and Heaven to follow a wretched, evil life by dint of a last minute rite.

Catholics would reply blandly, "Don't forget about Purgatory. He'll have to pay up." Our brethren would be scandalized all over again. A strange crew, Catholics.

The teaching is very simple. In the new Catechism of the Catholic Church:

> All who die in God's grace and friendship,
>> but still imperfectly purified,
>> are indeed assured of their eternal salvation;
>> but after death they undergo purification,
>> so as to achieve the holiness necessary to enter
>> the joy of heaven. (#1030)
> The Church gives the name *Purgatory*
>> to this final purification of the elect,
>> which is entirely different from the punishment of
>>> the damned. (#1031)
> From the beginning
>> the Church has honored the memory of the dead
>> and offered prayers in suffrage for them,
>> above all the Eucharistic sacrifice,
>> so that, thus purified
>> they may attain the beatific vision of God. (#1032)

We pray for our dead that they speedily find the fullness of life with God. We fear the judgment of God and do not presume too much, but support our hope by prayer for all the dead. For the average person prayer is enormous comfort and the best therapy in sorrow. Most Mass offerings sent here are for the dead, many for the poor souls, so-called— meaning all the dead.

We are all one community: the Church Triumphant, the Church Militant, the Church Suffering. Everyone living with us this hour on earth is our contemporary destined for Heaven as much as we, created by God, loved by God. We include all in our prayer. It is both privilege and duty.

St. Augustine's mother told him not to be concerned about where they buried her, just be sure to remember her at the altar.

We might in turn say, I really don't care what color you wear at my final rites. Just be sure the prayers are fervent.

For the Burial of a Monastery Worker's Mother

We wear white today, because white is for joy. The joy is the passing of a beautiful woman who led a beautiful life, to the realms of eternal beauty, to the Bosom of God.
Life at times seems a series of good-byes, of departures.

We leave the first home we knew, our mother's womb.
We leave the breasts we sucked.
We leave the childhood we knew
We leave the house we loved.
And all the leavings were both sadness and joy.

Who has not known the wrenching of the heart when we must say good-bye to someone we love, maybe never to see again?

Yet, for the Christian the joy is surpassing. We are destined for great things to come if we are willing to believe in them and show our belief one way or another.

Essie surely showed it in the way she lived. She took a vow and she kept it. Everyone who has ever made a vow knows how hard it can be. We fault no one, for we know how it is, but are all the more joyful when someone in the grace of God can fulfill it—for better and for worse, in sickness and in health, richer or poorer, till death do us part. Words easily spoken when you are young and naïve. Could she have known? Could she see down the road? And yet, and yet, she kept the word and nursed her love through decades of debilitating disease, with ten children. Talk to me of love. Tell me of dedication, and I'll tell you more.

The monks have had the folks for neighbors for a long time, north and south. One to the north was a great friend of Thomas Merton. His cousin to the south was the one with whom we had more to deal.

Essie worked for years as chef and hostess in our Family Guest House. She came to know the monks and their families.

The one who has worked for us since his teens told me that he never knew his father as a working man. He was already into Parkinson's. Yet that elder knew how to work in his day. He sure did. The sons, not to say the daughters, prove as much.

They were good neighbors. They got to know us and still loved us. Is not that the essence of a good neighbor?

She leaves a treasure to her ten children and her thirty-two grand-children and ten great grandchildren, not in monetary wealth, but in the real wealth of virtue. How grateful you should be! Do give thanks to God. Shed tears at her passing—who could help it?—but let those tears be graced with thanks to God for a great woman. Maybe that will move God to send us more of them.

Rest in peace, Essie. Yet I wish you more than peace. I pray you eternal rapture in the Bosom of God's love. Pray do not forget the rest of us on our way.

Funeral Mass for Brother Aelred

"Does God exact day-labor, light denied?"
I fondly ask. But Patience, to prevent
That murmur, soon replies, "God does not need
Either man's work or his own gifts. Who best
Bears his mild yoke, they serve him best. His state
Is kingly: thousands at his bidding speed,
And post o'er land and ocean without rest;
They also serve who only stand and wait."

Brother Aelred was born in Cleveland in 1915 of an Austrian migrant couple come over at the turn of the century. There were six boys and two girls. Only two girls are left, one eight-nine, one ninety, neither able to travel.

Aelred went to Holy Trinity Church and was an honor student at Cathedral Latin School. After graduation he entered Gethsemani at age eighteen in 1933 under Dom Edmond Obrecht. He was a bright, gentle, handsome young man.

Brother Aelred's life and death are the sort that test our faith very severely. On one level, his life makes no sense whatever. On another, his life may be more significant than that of any of us or all of us.

He first showed alarming signs of mental breakdown in 1941. He was in priestly studies with Father Augustine, a brilliant many-degreed scholar. He went as far as sub-diaconate, but got no further. He lived through Dom Frederic until 1948, Dom James till 1968, Dom Flavian till 1973, and the present abbot since. Most of that time he was in mental hospitals, but eventually a change was made and he came home with us when the new infirmary was finished, about twenty years ago. He was a paranoid schizophrenic, but any threat of violence had long since gone. The psychiatrist thought he had handled his disease remarkably well, said he lived a life of prayer. He rarely spoke, just sat in his chair. His mind was clear and sharp to the end.

A life of this kind tests our faith profoundly, for all its truly being a profound engagement with the mystery of salvation. I suggest it's better not to try to understand, but rather accept this mystery of God's providence. For all we know he may be the outstanding member of this community. Maybe he made Merton possible. Or you. Or me. It is dangerous to read the mind of God, and foolhardy to explain Him. After the Passion, Death, and Rising of His Son there is no telling any more how it works, how it adds up.

An encounter of this sort is not a specialty of monks. People everywhere cope with unfathomable mystery. Hopefully, in faith, they cope. They manage.

Hopefully, we will too. Perhaps more than that. Perhaps we can accept with thanks this strange interruption into our lives and hope that our response to it in faith may contribute to the cause—that is to say, the world's salvation in Christ.

That does not pretend to be an explanation, let alone some way of making the whole business something common sense can deal with— rather it is a call to faith, the soul of faith that stands bewildered before the mysteries of life and believes that somehow, some way, sometime or other, it will all come together in the beauty of love.

Brother Aelred's being among us these years is a call to that kind of faith for our own salvation and the salvation of the world.

May he now enjoy eternal glory and may he remain forever a monk of Gethsemani and be among us always in God's grace and love.

Father Thomas, nephew, you will tell his sisters Regina and Ottilia that we loved their brother very much.